"As followers of Christ, we've been given the power of the Holy Spirit to be a witness, share our faith, and turn our world upside down with the Gospel. All we have to do is receive it. In this book, my friend Sammy Rodriguez teaches you everything you need to know to be led, empowered by, and continually filled with the Holy Spirit."

Greg Laurie, senior pastor, Harvest Christian Fellowship

"When it comes to books on spiritual teaching, *Fresh Oil, Holy Fire, New Wine* is an instant classic! Pastor Sam Rodriguez is in a class of his own as he continues to elevate the hearts, minds, and spirits of readers across the world. This is a must-read for anyone who wants to go to the next level spiritually!"

DeVon Franklin, *New York Times* bestselling author

"This book is a profound guide to embracing the Holy Spirit's power and fullness. With clarity and passion, Pastor Samuel invites believers to tap into the transformative powers of the Holy Spirit while leaving believers encouraged to live boldly in the Spirit and experience a vibrant, fulfilling life of faith."

Russell Evans, senior pastor, Planetshakers

"As president of Oral Roberts University, I daily witness the deep hunger of new generations for authentic encounters and a sustained relationship with God. In his dynamic new book, Pastor Rodriquez takes us on a journey to discover a vibrant, supernatural relationship through the power of the Holy Spirit."

Dr. Billy Wilson, president, Oral Roberts University; global chair, Empowered21; chair, Pentecostal World Fellowship

"My good friend has done it again. This is an invaluable resource that reminds us that the Holy Spirit is not a ghost to be feared, not an *it* to be debated, not the idle member of the Trinity—He is the third person of the Godhead who lives inside born again Christians, and our relationship with Him is vital for spiritual growth and ministry effectiveness."

Doug Clay, general superintendent, Assemblies of God

FRESH OIL
HOLY FIRE
NEW WINE

Books by Samuel Rodriguez

LIVING THE VIBRANT
HOLY SPIRIT–FILLED LIFE

FRESH OIL
HOLY FIRE
NEW WINE

SAMUEL RODRIGUEZ

Chosen

a division of Baker Publishing Group
Minneapolis, Minnesota

Published by Chosen Books
Minneapolis, Minnesota
ChosenBooks.com

Chosen Books is a division of
Baker Publishing Group, Grand Rapids, Michigan

Printed in the United States of America

Library of Congress Cataloging-in-Publication Data
Names: Rodriguez, Samuel, author.
Title: Fresh oil, holy fire, new wine : living the vibrant Holy Spirit-filled life / Samuel Rodriguez.
Description: Minneapolis, Minnesota : Chosen Books, a division of Baker Publishing Group, [2024] | Includes bibliographical references
Identifiers: LCCN 2023053927 | ISBN 9780800763015 (cloth) | ISBN 9781493440856 (ebook)
Subjects: LCSH: Anointing of the Holy Spirit. | Holy Spirit. | Christian life.
Classification: LCC BT123 .R63 2024 | DDC 234/.13—dc23/eng/20240205
LC record available at https://lccn.loc.gov/2023053927

I dedicate this book to Bishop Tim Bagwell.
In Denver, Colorado, under the anointing of the Lord,
Pastor Bagwell released the title of this book to me,
not privy to the fact that the initial framework for the
manuscript occupied space on my phone.
That amazing confirmation solidified the clarion call
to release this message for such a time as this.

CONTENTS

FOREWORD

Having seen Samuel Rodriguez preach and speak on several occasions, it has become clear to me that the reason he speaks with such authority and power is that he has spent time in God's presence and His Word. Sammy's ability to weave together the truths found in the Bible with the ever-changing events of the modern day makes him relevant across all cultures, and it's also what makes *Fresh Oil, Holy Fire, New Wine* so special. Once again, Sammy has identified that what is needed most in a world gone mad isn't new programs or national strategies—it's the power and presence of the Holy Spirit and a move of God on His people.

As we approach the issues we face today and the forces of evil marshalled against us from shore to shore, we can have no greater hope than a holy fire from above, a powerful move of the Holy Spirit in and through His people, and a fresh word. *Fresh Oil, Holy Fire, New Wine* is that *rhema* word. Breakthroughs are here for everyone who reads this book. Renewed energy and excitement are waiting on every page, and revelation is coming to the life of each person who sits under this teaching from one of the most gifted communicators of our time.

Jentezen Franklin
Senior pastor, Free Chapel
New York Times bestselling author

1

THE SAME SPIRIT

Transformed by Faith, Fire, and Favor

The same Spirit that raised Christ from the dead is the same Spirit dwelling in you.
What you've been through has prepared you for what God is about to ignite in you.

In order to start a fire, you need fuel, heat, and oxygen. These elements may take different forms depending on the kind of fire ignited, but the fundamental ingredients remain the same. With a campfire, for instance, you usually gather twigs, sticks, and dry wood for fuel, use a match or lighter to apply heat, and rely on the open air of the great outdoors to ensure adequate oxygen. While this kind of fire is intentional and contained, accidental fires burning out of control rely on the same elements. Not long ago my wife, Eva, and I confronted this phenomenon when we thought our house was burning down.

I had just returned from a trip, and Eva was baking something delicious in the oven. The smell that met me was a wonderful welcome home. She walked out of the kitchen and came to greet me, helping me unload my bags so that we could hug. Although I was exhausted from traveling, my mind was still going a million miles an hour with various and assorted incidents, anecdotes, and ideas that I couldn't wait to share with my wife.

As Eva relayed how our kids and grandkids were doing, we both suddenly smelled something burning. She raced into the kitchen and immediately shouted, "SAM!" Entering the room, I saw flames shooting out of the oven and spreading to counter items on either side.

While Eva frantically beat at the growing flames with a dish towel, I looked under the sink for our fire extinguisher, which to my great dismay was empty. Forgetting all my knowledge of how to extinguish a kitchen fire safely, I did the worst thing possible—I threw a pan of water on the flames!

As steam from my attempt mixed with smoke, a fireball erupted as if a volcano was about to erupt. My thoughts at that moment were getting Eva out of the house and wondering whether I would have time to grab important papers and family photos. Ushering my wife out the front door, I dialed 911 on my phone and hoped I could hear the dispatch operator through the shrill beeping of the smoke alarm overhead.

A smoky cloud trailed behind us through the open door, but as soon as it dissipated, the air cleared. Confused, I rushed back into our kitchen and could not believe my eyes. The fire had completely extinguished itself—leaving no damage! The stovetop looked wet and messy from my failed attempt to douse the flames, but the counters were not even singed. Lingering wisps of smoke rose, but it was as if the fire had never happened.

The science geek in me analyzed what I had just experienced. I concluded that opening our front door had sent a burst of air into the kitchen that basically smothered the fire with too much oxygen. Or perhaps the counters were indeed heat resistant, leaving the flames with no fuel. I even wondered if my panful of water had worked after all.

The Spirit-led believer that I am, however, knew better. One of those explanations might describe what happened, but the truth hit me as I recalled a couple of messages I had received in the previous 24 hours. The night before, I had received a text message from one of my friends I hadn't talked with in a while. "Pastor Sam, for whatever reason, I am praying for a supernatural hedge of protection." I thanked him, and we made a plan to catch up. And that very morning, I had received another text from a different friend. "Sam, I'm praying for protection right now. God's going before you. Everything's going to be fine."

At the time, I was grateful for these messages and encouraged by my friends' prayers of protection. But standing there in our kitchen, I had no doubt the Holy Spirit had compelled these friends to lift me up, pray for my safety, and communicate their concern. Because one moment the oven had been overflowing with fire and smoke like a mini-Vesuvius, and the next it was mysteriously extinguished. I prayed a prayer of gratitude and thanksgiving, smiling at the knowledge that what the Spirit foretold, God fulfilled.

Fire Power

That experience reminds me not only of the ingredients necessary to sustain a fire but of what's required to experience spiritual combustion in us. As we learned from our kitchen fire, having fuel and oxygen isn't enough for a fire to grow without a sustainable source of heat. Which is why Jesus sent His Spirit to dwell in us—to ignite God's power within us.

It's no coincidence that the gift of the Holy Spirit appeared incendiary when it first descended upon believers. "Then, what looked like flames or tongues of fire appeared and settled on each of them. And everyone present was filled with the Holy Spirit" (Acts 2:3–4 NLT). The timing and appearance of the Spirit's arrival may have surprised these early believers, but they knew they were about to experience something transformative.

Jesus had prepared His followers for this gift prior to His death and resurrection. "And I will ask the Father, and he will give you another advocate to help you and be with you forever—the Spirit of truth" (John 14:16–17). After Christ rose from the dead, He once again promised them this gift and commanded them not to leave Jerusalem until they received it. "John baptized with water, but in just a few days you will be baptized with the Holy Spirit" (Acts 1:5 NLT). Finally, just moments before His ascension, Jesus explained,

> But you will receive power when the Holy Spirit comes upon you. And you will be my witnesses, telling people about me everywhere—in Jerusalem, throughout Judea, in Samaria, and to the ends of the earth.
>
> Acts 1:8 NLT

After they heard these words from their Master, the disciples watched Christ ascend into a cloud (see Acts 1:9).

Despite anticipating the gift of the Spirit and receiving His indwelling presence at Pentecost, these early believers discovered that the Spirit's impact changed the way they related to God and to everyone around them. They had to live out the answer to Paul's rhetorical question in his letter to the Christians at Corinth: "Don't you know that you yourselves are God's temple and that God's Spirit dwells in your midst?" (1 Corinthians 3:16).

Knowing you have power is not the same as accessing that power.

If we have invited God's Spirit to dwell in us and have chosen to follow Jesus, then we are also compelled to answer this query for ourselves. Because knowing you have power is not the same as accessing that power. And accessing that power requires knowing how to use it.

When our hearts are ignited by the presence of the Holy Spirit, everything changes.

Power, Not Potential

This process can be similar to driving a car. The basic premise of operating an automotive vehicle requires learning how to negotiate the power of its engine. You can know all about the internal combustion process, how burning gasoline gets converted into torque that causes pistons to go up and down in the cylinders, which then powers the driveshaft to turn the wheels. You may be capable of popping the hood and identifying various parts and components—the radiator, battery, spark plugs, and intake valves.

But your awareness and operational knowledge is not enough.

Understanding an automotive engine will not transport you from one point to another, allow you to drive across town, or empower your next road trip. Potential is not the same as power. To harness the power of that engine and operate the car, you must get in, ignite the engine, and shift the transmission. You have to know how to accelerate, brake, and read the various indicators and dash screens. You must learn to navigate among unique, ever-changing variables—including weather, traffic, construction, accidents, and detours—and adjust as necessary to proceed and reach your destination.

As followers of Jesus, we can find ourselves in a similar situation.

We know we have the Holy Spirit dwelling inside us. We know there is nothing and no one more powerful than God. And yet we often struggle to access this unlimited holy power within us. We struggle to experience the life of abundance Jesus said He came to bring, to live in the fulfillment of the peace, purpose, and power God provides, and to be a conduit of healing power, transforming love, and unfathomable grace.

We have more power than we can possibly imagine. But we may not be relying on that power to get us from our mess to our miracle.

We may know *about* the Holy Spirit but not know Him *personally*.

We believe in God and seek Him in all areas of our lives but still rely on ourselves.

We feel frustrated knowing that there has to be more but not sure how to experience it.

If any of these statements resonate with you, then I have good news, my friend. I felt convicted to write this book to help you experience the engine of faith in your life, God's Spirit in you, so that His power can further transform you and the way you live: to comfort and console you, to equip and empower you, to beckon and befriend you, to encourage and enliven you.

If you're struggling in your faith, wondering how to align what you know to be true from the pages of God's Word with the reality of what you're experiencing on a daily basis, then I hope I can help you close that gap. My prayer is that you can come to know, embrace, and enjoy the fullness of living in the power of the Holy Spirit—*every moment of every day.*

So often we pray for power and yet fear the very power God has already placed within us. We want more but settle for less. We hope but grow weary. We give in to temptation and struggle to get back on our feet. We feel blindsided by the enemy even as we try to see with the eyes of our heart. We seek to eliminate our weaknesses rather than allow God's strength to heal and empower us through them.

It's time to experience what's already in you—the resurrection power of Jesus.

Spiritual Combustion

The authority of the truth of this fact does not reside in my being a pastor. It does not reside on my own experience, as revealing and evident as it may be. It is not based on superstition, supposition, or suggestion. The authority on the truth that divine resurrection power resides in you comes directly from the Word of God. "The Spirit of God, who raised Jesus from the dead, lives in you" (Romans 8:11 NLT).

This statement is the centerpiece and thesis of Romans 8. Paul wrote this letter to the believers in Rome to help them understand the gift they received when they accepted God's grace-gift of salvation through the death and resurrection of His Son, Jesus Christ. He wanted to make sure they realize the change that had already occurred within them so that they could convert from their previous ways of thinking, speaking, and behaving to their new Spirit-based way of living. They no longer had to try harder—they simply had to recognize the power within.

This power is not simply a onetime occurrence—the Spirit is the gift that keeps on giving! Because the same Spirit that defeated death and resurrected the corpse of the crucified Jesus lying in the borrowed tomb sealed by an enormous boulder, the same Spirit that ignited the restoration and renewal of life in the lifeless body of our Lord, is the same Spirit you have been given.

> This power is not simply a onetime occurrence—the Spirit is the gift that keeps on giving!

Let's consider the direct implications here. If the Spirit of God, who raised Jesus from the dead, lives in you, then so what? What does this mean exactly? What's the big deal about the Spirit working more than two thousand years ago in a cave-carved tomb in Jerusalem being the same Spirit working right now at this very moment inside you?

The big deal is this: *If Jesus overcame, you can overcome.*

What did we learn from the resurrection? We learned that if Jesus can come back to life after the violent, brutal, torturous death He experienced, a government-sanctioned execution for common criminals, then you can come out of anything.

Anything.

The same Spirit that raised Jesus from the dead—yes, *that* Spirit, He is the same One living inside you right now. How is this possible? Well, are you born again? Are you a Christ follower? Did you confess with your mouth and do you believe in your heart that Jesus is the Lord and Savior of your life? Do you love the Lord your God with all your heart, with all your soul, with all your strength, and with all your mind (see Luke 10:27)?

If your answer is yes to these queries, then you must understand that you do not have a counterfeit spirit, an outdated version, an old operating system, a basic model that's less powerful. What you have in you is not a clone, not a cheap imitation, not a replica, not a Times Square forty-dollar knockoff. Not a diluted spirit, a watered-down version, a leftover to be reheated, a flickering ember from what was once a mighty fire.

No, my friend, you have the same living Spirit of God that raised Jesus inside you right now. The same unique, empowering, emancipating, elevating Spirit that resurrected Christ lives—not visits, hovers, or drifts in and out—resides, occupies, dwells, and inhabits *you*.

What Spirit are we talking about? *The* same Spirit.

Which Spirit is this? The *same* Spirit.

They're the same, really? Yes, the same *Spirit*.

The same Spirit that hovered and covered the chaotic waters at the beginning of Creation lives inside you. "The earth was formless and empty, and darkness covered the deep waters. And the Spirit of God was hovering over the surface of the waters" (Genesis 1:2 NLT). Think about this scene for a moment. The Spirit hovered and covered a mess until God said, "Let there be light" (Genesis 1:3 NLT) and kept creating from there.

Isn't it amazing that we serve a God who hovers and covers us even when we are messy, raw, in progress, unfinished, and uncertain? He hovers and covers us until we are ready to receive His Spirit and run with His word for us. Having this same Spirit prepares us for the new creation He's bringing forth in us, for the illumination of His light entering our lives.

What does this mean?

God's Spirit covers your mess until you're ready to step into His miracle.

What you've been through has prepared you for what God is about to ignite in you!

Oil Spill

If the same Spirit that raised Jesus from the grave dwells in you—and He does—then it's time to turn your potential into power. If you're stuck, it's time to get unstuck. If you're plodding along, it's time to pick up the pace. If you're not sure of your direction, then it's time to confirm your destination.

How can you experience the dynamic Spirit-led, Spirit-filled, Spirit-fueled life that God has for you? While we find numerous references and descriptors for God's Spirit throughout the Bible, three stand out to express your spiritual growth—fresh oil, holy fire, and new wine. These three serve as biblical symbols of the Holy Spirit's presence, power, and purpose in our lives.

Why these three in particular? And what relevance do they singularly and cumulatively have on your life right now? That's what this book is all about! I will briefly explain here, and then the concepts will be explored in more depth on the following pages.

Fresh oil is about your anointing.

Throughout Scripture, in both the Old and the New Testaments, anointing with oil symbolizes God's presence, power, and purpose on people and places set apart as holy and chosen. God gave Moses the specific recipe for mixing anointing oil, which included myrrh, cinnamon, and other natural ingredients added to olive oil (see Exodus 30:22–24). Anointing oil was poured lightly on the heads of high priests, kings, and other leaders to indicate their status as God's chosen representatives to His people. The same sacred blend was also sprinkled in the Tabernacle on various items, including the Ark of the Covenant, and various tables, lamps, and altars (see Exodus 30:26–29).

In the life of David, the shepherd boy who grew into a man after God's own heart, we notice he was anointed three different times. The first occasion occurred when God's prophet Samuel, following the Lord's instructions, went in search of King Saul's successor to the throne of Israel. "So Samuel took the horn of oil and anointed him in the presence of his brothers, and from that day on the Spirit of the Lord came powerfully upon David" (1 Samuel 16:13). This was the anointment of assignment.

The second took place following Saul's death when the men of Judah anointed David as the new king over the house of Judah (see 2 Samuel 2:4). This anointing was about acceptance—accepting change, accepting the present over the past, accepting the cost of his calling. David's passion to lead and his willingness to embrace God's purpose for his life emerged out of this anointing.

David's third anointing was one of advancement. "When all the elders of Israel had come to King David at Hebron, the king made a covenant with them at Hebron before the Lord, and they anointed David king over Israel" (2 Samuel 5:3). Finally, all of the tribes of Israel united under David's sovereignty as God's chosen leader. And with this kind of unity, David led his men to defeat the Jebusites and to capture Zion, now known as the City of David (see 2 Samuel 5:6–7).

Drawing on David's example, we see how God anoints our purpose, then He anoints our passion, and then He anoints our promise. Each of these anointings through the grace-filled finished work of Jesus equips, instructs, and releases upon us a measurable impartation that will enable us to shine with the glory of Christ in our respective generations. And for us today, fresh oil doesn't require an herbal recipe—because we are anointed by the Holy Spirit.

> **God anoints our purpose, then He anoints our passion, and then He anoints our promise.**

In the Old Testament, when people were anointed, the oil placed on the outside represented God's presence on the inside. They were anointed from the outside in. When Jesus died on the cross, rose from the dead, and sent the gift of His Holy Spirit, He flipped the script on anointing. When we are born again, we are no longer anointed from the outside in—we are anointed from the *inside out.*

Your power does not derive from an external variable. Your power emerges out of an internal constant.

22

Because the anointing lives inside of you, greater is he that is in you than he that is in the world (see 1 John 4:4).

Because the anointing lives inside of you, out of your belly shall flow rivers of living water (see John 7:38).

Your anointing is when the Holy Spirit inside of you works through you to change the world around you. "The Spirit of the Lord is on me, because he has anointed me to proclaim good news to the poor. He has sent me to proclaim freedom for the prisoners and recovery of sight for the blind, to set the oppressed free" (Luke 4:18).

From Genesis to Revelation, we find that God anoints what He will use for His glory. To be anointed is to be separated, put aside, for God's usage. God anoints people. God anoints places. God anoints things. And God anoints seasons.

There is a fresh anointing coming upon you.

There is a fresh anointing coming upon your household.

There is a fresh anointing coming upon the new season before you.

David was anointed three times, in three different seasons, affirming his kingship. Yet every single time he was anointed, the consensus regarding his divine favor multiplied. He was able to occupy and conquer more, every single time he was anointed.

God has fresh oil for you, and fresh oil means a fresh anointing. Your fresh anointing means that you are about to experience the fulfillment of new promises, occupy more roles, conquer larger territories, and enjoy greater favor while having more influence for the glory of Jesus than ever before.

Fresh oil is about your anointing—your assignment, your acceptance, your advancement.

Fire Proof

You're also stepping into a season not just of fresh oil but of holy fire.

Before the Spirit descended on believers at Pentecost in tongues of flame (see Acts 2:3–4), Jesus had foretold that holy fire was coming.

23

"He will baptize you with the Holy Spirit and fire" (Matthew 3:11). Simply put, holy fire is the unlimited, unquenchable power of the Holy Spirit. The fire of God is the presence of God. "God is a consuming fire" (Hebrews 12:29). This is not a new description of the Spirit's power and presence, but one we find burning throughout the Old and New Testaments.

When God first appeared to Moses in the book of Exodus, He revealed Himself as a blazing bush. "There the angel of the LORD appeared to him in flames of fire from within a bush. Moses saw that though the bush was on fire it did not burn up" (Exodus 3:2). The Lord also accompanied the Israelites out of Egypt through the desert into the Promised Land as a pillar of fire. "By day the LORD went ahead of them in a pillar of cloud to guide them on their way and by night in a pillar of fire to give them light, so that they could travel by day or night" (Exodus 13:21).

Elijah prayed and holy fire came down (see 2 Kings 1:10).

Three Hebrew boys, Hebrew captives in Babylon who refused to renounce their faith in God, experienced holy fire the moment the fourth man showed up in the furnace (see Daniel 3:8–25).

Jeremiah said he couldn't stop preaching because he had what could only be described as holy fire shut up in his bones (see Jeremiah 20:9).

The holy fire of God is a sanctifying fire, a purifying fire, a consuming fire that will address and remove once and for all every vestige of toxicity, every lie of the enemy, every obstacle and impediment to the fulfillment of God's purpose in your life. Unexpected vipers may strike and latch on, but they will never survive holy fire (see Acts 28:3–5).

For the believer, holy fire will not punish you—it will protect you.

You need to get ready for the pilot light burning within you to blaze into a conflagration of God's power in your life. You need to get ready for holy fire power. You should expect God to show up in you, with you, for you, and through you like never before.

Don't be afraid of this fire, don't douse it with water, and don't grab a fire extinguisher. It's time to welcome holy fire in your life!

Wine Tasting

When you experience fresh oil and holy fire—your anointing and empowerment through the same Spirit that resurrected Jesus from the dead—you enter into a season of new wine. The prophet Amos offers a description in God's Decree that resonates His promise for you and me today.

> Yes indeed, it won't be long now. Things are going to happen so fast your head will swim, one thing fast on the heels of the other. You won't be able to keep up. Everything will be happening at once—and everywhere you look, blessings! Blessings like wine pouring off the mountains and hills.
>
> Amos 9:13–15 MSG

It's no coincidence that Jesus blessed wine on the night before His death and instructed His disciples to drink it in remembrance of Him. "This wine is my blood, which will be poured out to forgive the sins of many and begin the new agreement from God to his people" (Matthew 26:28 ERV). When we partake of Communion today, we continue this sacred commemoration.

It's no coincidence that at Pentecost, when Spirit-filled believers began speaking in various languages all at once, others mistakenly assumed they were drunk with wine (see Acts 2:13). But Peter wasted no time clarifying their misperception. He not only wanted to set the record straight about the cause of their speech, but he also wanted to take the opportunity with a crowd gathered to make a direct connection to the past, to Jewish prophecy that was being fulfilled before their very eyes.

> Then Peter stepped forward with the eleven other apostles and shouted to the crowd, "Listen carefully, all of you, fellow Jews and residents of Jerusalem! Make no mistake about this. These people are not drunk, as some of you are assuming. Nine o'clock in the

morning is much too early for that. No, what you see was predicted long ago by the prophet Joel:

'In the last days,' God says,
 'I will pour out my Spirit upon all people.
Your sons and daughters will prophesy.
 Your young men will see visions,
 and your old men will dream dreams.
In those days I will pour out my Spirit
 even on my servants—men and women alike—
 and they will prophesy.
And I will cause wonders in the heavens above
 and signs on the earth below—
 blood and fire and clouds of smoke.
The sun will become dark,
 and the moon will turn blood red
 before that great and glorious day of the LORD arrives.
But everyone who calls on the name of the LORD
 will be saved.'"

Acts 2:14–21 NLT

While the believers at Pentecost were not drunk with wine but filled with the Spirit, they had nonetheless tasted the new wine of Christ's blood shed for them on the cross. Indeed, Jesus may have foreshadowed the filling of the Holy Spirit that His followers experienced after His resurrection when He said, "And no one puts new wine into old wineskins. For the old skins would burst from the pressure, spilling the wine and ruining the skins. New wine is stored in new wineskins so that both are preserved" (Matthew 9:17 NLT).

When you have Jesus, you are no longer who you were in the past—you are a new creature in Christ. When you welcome Jesus into your heart, you need to recognize the need for change. New wine requires new wineskins. When you are filled by the Holy Spirit, you cannot expect to act as you once did.

You cannot expect to relate as you once did.
You cannot expect to love as you once did.
You cannot expect to work as you once did.
You cannot expect to play as you once did.
You cannot expect to worship as you once did.
You cannot expect to praise as you once did.

Abiding in the same Spirit that raised Jesus from the dead means a fresh start, a clean slate. You are a new creature in Christ who has been washed white as snow by the blood of the Lamb. You have a new life in the power and freedom of God's Spirit. Your life will never be the same!

Fresh, Holy, New

The same Spirit that raised Jesus from the dead dwells in you.
The same Spirit that anointed David with fresh oil anoints you.
The same Spirit that ignited believers at Pentecost burns in you.
The same Spirit that has shown favor to God's followers now blesses you.

You are stepping into a season of fresh oil, holy fire, and new wine in order to experience the Spirit-filled life at the next level. You are receiving fresh oil, holy fire, and new wine to get back everything that was lost. Everything that was stolen, corrupted, and held back.

You're getting back all you've lost—and more.
You're getting your joy back.
You're getting your peace back.
You're getting your family back.
You're getting your health back.
God wants to anoint you for what's next with fresh oil.
God wants to empower you for what's next with holy fire.
God wants to bless you for what's next with new wine.
The source for your fresh oil, holy fire, and new wine?

The same Spirit that raised Christ from the dead!

There's no better declaration of what you can expect next than what Paul wrote to the church at Philippi: "I want to know Christ and experience the mighty power that raised him from the dead" (Philippians 3:10 NLT). Knowing Jesus allows you to access the same power source that defeated death and restored life. There's no mistake—this Spirit is one and the same as who is in you.

The same Spirit that brought Jesus out of the tomb is more than powerful enough to take you out of the worst season and into the best season, from death to life.

The same Spirit of the Lord is upon you in power.

To every Joseph with a dream, you're not in the pit anymore.

To every Moses with a past, you're not in Egypt anymore.

To every Joshua with a milk-and-honey vision, you're not in the desert anymore.

To every Ruth and Naomi, you're not in Moab anymore.

To every Shadrach, Meshack, and Abednego, you're not in the furnace anymore.

To every Peter and John, Paul and Silas, you're not in prison anymore.

To every Lazarus buried alive, you're not in the tomb anymore.

No matter where you are or what you're facing, you have the same Spirit.

Through the resurrection power of the same Spirit, get ready to experience fresh oil, holy fire, and new wine.

THE SAME SPIRIT IN YOU

At the end of each chapter, you will find a few questions to help you reflect on the main points covered and think about how they apply to your life. These should not feel like homework or a burden, but rather a way to enhance your experience and give you space to listen for how God may want to speak to you. While you don't have to write down your responses, you might be surprised to discover how helpful it can be to keep a record of your experience with the Spirit as you read each chapter.

Whether you record your answers or not, after you've spent a few moments thinking through these questions, I encourage you to go to the Lord in prayer and share with Him what's going on in your heart. Begin a new conversation with the Holy Spirit inside you. To help ignite your conversation with God, you'll find a short prayer to spark your communication with Him. Remember that no matter what you're facing, you have the same Spirit that raised Jesus from the dead living in you.

1. How would you describe your relationship with the Holy Spirit up until this point? What's the basis for your description?

2. How have you experienced anointing in your life so far? Which of the three anointings in David's life—assignment, acceptance, or advancement—is next for you?

3. What empty tombs have you left behind through the resurrection power of the same Spirit in you? How has God's power changed your life from who and where you used to be?

Dear God, thank You for the incredible gift of Your Holy Spirit dwelling in me! Help me to grasp all the implications of having the same Spirit that raised Jesus from the dead residing within me. I welcome Your power and all that You want to reveal to me within these pages. Remove my fears, my anxieties, my worries, and my distractions so that I can fix the eyes of my heart on Jesus and experience the Spirit's resurrection power like never before. Remind me of Your unmovable, unshakable, constant presence in my life as my firm foundation, my Rock of Ages. May Your Spirit allow me to know You more fully as I experience Your fresh oil, holy fire, and new wine in my life. In Jesus' name, Amen.

PART 1

HEAD

Informed by the Spirit

So if there is any encouragement in Christ, any comfort from love, any participation in the Spirit, any affection and sympathy, complete my joy by being of the same mind, having the same love, being in full accord and of one mind.

Philippians 2:1–2 ESV

2

HOLY DYNAMITE

Igniting the Same Spirit

The Holy Spirit is the greatest empowering force in the universe!
The most powerful people on planet earth are those filled with the Holy Spirit!

W hat comes to mind when you think of dynamite? Depending on your age and generation, you might immediately see a cartoon image pop into your thoughts, a red cylinder with a fuse trailing one end, ignited and sparkling. You know, the kind Wile E. Coyote used unsuccessfully in his quest to stop the Road Runner. Often ordered from the fictionally generic Acme Company, the Coyote's cartoon dynamite never worked the way he wanted. His explosive traps always backfired so that the dynamite detonated on the conniving canine and not the sly speedster.

Along the same pop-culture train of thought, you might think of *Napoleon Dynamite*, the 2004 independent comedy film about an awkward young man's coming-of-age experiences over the course of his junior year in high school. The film is known for its wry, deadpan delivery of Napoleon's commentary about life's absurdities based on the ludicrous situations and quirky characters he encounters. Non sequiturs abound, but some critics, along with many millennial fans, revere it as one of the funniest movies of all time.

If cartoons and comedies aren't where your mind goes when you think about dynamite, you might have had a more academic response. As someone intrigued by history and science, you might have thought of Alfred Nobel, the brainy namesake of the prestigious Nobel Prizes and inventor of dynamite.

Born in 1833 in Stockholm, Nobel grew up mentored by his father, a construction engineer and inventor continually searching for more efficient ways to demolish rocks and other obstacles at building sites. As a young man, Alfred Nobel also served as a protégé of Ascanio Sobrero, an Italian chemist who invented nitroglycerine. It was considered of little practical value, however, because of its liquid volatility.

With his father's construction business in mind, Nobel set about finding a way to make nitroglycerine controllable and commercially viable. He spent years trying different combinations and survived several accidental explosions, including one that killed Alfred's brother, Emil. Consequently, local officials banned further experiments within their jurisdiction.

Determined that Emil's death would not be in vain, Nobel persevered in more remote locales, eventually mixing nitroglycerine with powdery sand to form a solid paste that could be rolled into rods. He then created blasting caps with fuses that could be attached to the rods for detonation. After years of costly trial and error, in 1887 Nobel finally filed for a patent for his new invention that he named "dynamite," based on the Greek word for great power, *dunamis*.[1]

Since then, dynamite has become a mainstay in construction, mining, and demolition—as well as Looney Tunes cartoons and nerdy comedies.

The Promise of Power

There's one more critical association with dynamite that I would be remiss if I didn't share with you. This association has an even greater impact than Nobel's invention because its application pertains directly to you. My hope is that anytime you hear or see the word *dynamite* from now on, you will immediately think of God's power in you.

You see, not only does the Holy Spirit reveal Himself through the anointing of fresh oil, the presence of holy fire, and the blessing of new wine, but the gift of the Holy Spirit is spiritual dynamite! After Christ rose from the dead—empowered by the same Spirit that's within you—He spent some time with His followers and friends making sure they knew He was, indeed, alive again.

> During the forty days after he suffered and died, he appeared to the apostles from time to time, and he proved to them in many ways that he was actually alive. And he talked to them about the Kingdom of God.
>
> Acts 1:3 NLT

Jesus also promised them a gift and commanded them not to leave Jerusalem until they received it. "John baptized with water," Christ told them, "but in just a few days you will be baptized with the Holy Spirit" (verse 5 NLT). Now the disciples had a context for recalling the way John the Baptist would immerse people in the Jordan River after they came looking for him, confessed their sins, and acknowledged repentance (see Matthew 3:1–17).

Jesus had gone to John and been baptized. The gift that Jesus referenced was revealed as soon as He came up out of the water. "At that moment heaven was opened, and he saw the Spirit of God descending like a dove and alighting on him. And a voice from heaven said, 'This is my Son, whom I love; with him I am well pleased'" (Matthew 3:16–17). Other than this scene, we might wonder if the disciples grasped what Jesus was describing. Perhaps they thought they would soon be enveloped by doves descending from heaven!

Regardless of what they expected, they were eager to receive this intriguing gift Jesus promised. A bit like kids who persist in wanting to know when they can open their presents, the disciples kept asking Jesus about the timing of His departure—and presumably the arrival of their gift—and He made it clear that the Father alone knew that schedule.

Nonetheless, Jesus tried to prepare them for life after He left their midst in person, explaining, "But you will receive power when the Holy Spirit comes upon you. And you will be my witnesses, telling people about me everywhere—in Jerusalem, throughout Judea, in Samaria, and to the ends of the earth" (Acts 1:8 NLT). After they heard these words from their Master, the disciples watched Christ ascend into a cloud (see verse 9).

What did Jesus say would be coming?

What's this unique gift that you will receive?

You will receive a dove?

You will receive hot-and-cold tingles?

You will receive a shake?

You will receive a quake?

You will receive an emotion?

You will receive an opinion?

You will receive a feeling?

You will receive a religion?

No—none of the above!

Jesus said, "You will receive *power*!"

Divine Dynamite

This promise of power following His resurrection was not the first time Jesus had foretold the gift of the Spirit to come. Before He was arrested and crucified, Jesus had taught in the Temple courts in Jerusalem during the Festival of Tabernacles (see John 7:2, 14). There, He proclaimed, "Believe in me so that rivers of living water will burst out from within you, flowing from your innermost being, just like the Scripture says!" (John 7:38 TPT). Just to be sure Christ's reference was clear, John, when later writing his gospel, explained, "Jesus was prophesying about the Holy Spirit that believers were being prepared to receive" (John 7:39 TPT).

You'll recall that Jesus had offered this living water to the Samaritan woman at the well (see John 4). And since they were at the place where drinking water was drawn, we might have assumed that this living water was like a cool, refreshing gulp on a hot, dusty day. And most likely there's nothing wrong or inaccurate about making this assumption.

But the way Jesus described living water at the Festival of Tabernacles was not drawn from a well, poured from a bucket, or sipped from a cup. No, He said, "Believe in Me." Notice the consequence of placing your faith in Jesus Christ, the Son of God: "So that rivers of living water will burst out from within you, flowing from your innermost being."

This wellspring within you flows in rivers that will burst out. We're not talking about a drinking fountain, garden hose, or fire hydrant.

We're talking about the mighty Mississippi flooding its banks.

We're talking about the Colorado River bursting through the Hoover Dam.

We're talking about rivers—notice the plural—bursting out from within you.

Not trickling or dripping.

Not sprinkling or pouring.

Not squirting or misting.

Rivers of living water bursting out!

My friend, this kind of power cannot be comprehensively described by comparing it to water as we know it. Even as Jesus compares the Holy Spirit to this limitless geyser of living water within you, the focus is on the power. The kind of power that descended upon Jesus in the Jordan on the day He was baptized (see Matthew 3:16).

This is the kind of power to move mountains (see Matthew 17:20) and to speak into the storm, declaring, "Quiet! Be still!" (Mark 4:39).

This is the kind of power to speak life into friends and followers, commanding Lazarus to come forth, Zacchaeus to come down, and the Samaritan woman at the well to go and sin no more.

This is the kind of power to cast out devils and demons, knowing full well that you are protected from harm. "I have **This kind** given you authority to trample on snakes and scor- **of power** pions and to overcome all the power of the enemy; **is divine** nothing will harm you" (Luke 10:19). **dynamite!** This is the kind of power to confront every work of the enemy in front of you attempting to stop the fulfillment of your God-ordained purpose. The kind of power to say, "Get behind me, Satan! You are a stumbling block to me" (Matthew 16:23).

This is the kind of power that is divine dynamite!

Three Times the Power

Long before Alfred Nobel coined the name *dynamite* for his explosive invention, the apostle Paul lit a fuse on our understanding of spiritual power by using the same root word, *dunamis*. In fact, Paul helps us grasp not only one kind, but *three* kinds of power we have available to us through the Holy Spirit. Writing to the believers at Ephesus, Paul shared his prayer requests for his brothers and sisters in Christ.

I pray that you will continually experience the immeasurable greatness of God's power made available to you through faith. Then your lives will be an advertisement of this immense power as it works through you! This is the mighty power that was released when God raised Christ from the dead and exalted him to the place of highest honor and supreme authority in the heavenly realm! And now he is exalted as first above every ruler, authority, government, and realm of power in existence! He is gloriously enthroned over every name that is ever praised, not only in this age, but in the age that is coming!

Ephesians 1:19–21 TPT

Notice how many times the word *power* occurs in this passage. If you counted four, you're correct—at least until we look closer at the original Greek words Paul chose. While those Greek words are all rendered as "power," here and in many other Bible translations, we find three distinct kinds of power mentioned. Perhaps it would be helpful to show you what I'm talking about by breaking out each verse and including the original words:

> I pray that you will continually experience the immeasurable greatness of God's POWER (*dunamis*) made available to you through faith. Then your lives will be an advertisement of this immense POWER (*dunamis*) as it works through you! This is the mighty POWER (*kratos*) that was released when God raised Christ from the dead and exalted him to the place of highest honor and supreme authority in the heavenly realm! And now he is exalted as first above every ruler, authority, government, and realm of POWER (*exusia*) in existence! He is gloriously enthroned over every name that is ever praised, not only in this age, but in the age that is coming!

So you see, Paul refers to three distinct types or expressions of power, beginning with *dunamis*. This *dunamis* power is the kind that inspired Nobel to name his invention dynamite. *Dunamis* power explodes with miraculous and unlimited force. This is the vested and inherent power of God in us through the indwelling of the Holy Spirit—the same Spirit that exploded with life to resurrect the dead body of Jesus in the tomb. *Dunamis* is positional power, based on inherent proximity and location. Because of who you are in Christ, and because Christ is in you, you have unimaginable, indescribable, unfathomable heavenly power. Or, as I like to call it, holy dynamite!

While the same Spirit is our source for *dunamis* power, God's Word also tells us that it derives from the essence of the Gospel. "The message of the cross is foolishness to those who are perishing, but to us who are being saved it is the power of God" (1 Corinthians 1:18).

While *dunamis* lies within you and is not usually visible to human eyes, the next kind of power mentioned by Paul, *kratos*, is the exhibition or expression of that divine power within, often in the form of visible dominion and rule. *Kratos* power explodes with *dunamis* power, allowing you to take action and experience visible results. Or consider it this way: If *dunamis* power is living water, then *kratos* is bursting forth out of those rivers of living water within you. *Dunamis* is your source, and *kratos* enables you to draw on it in order to bring life from death, order from chaos, and light from darkness.

When you exercise *kratos* power, you are standing strong and not budging an inch for the enemy. You refuse to surrender your territory, and you never retreat. You do not give up on your God-given dream. You do not give up on your family. You do not give up on your future. You know that the *dunamis* power—the same Spirit that raised Christ from the dead—lives in you, which means you are an overcomer, a death-defying divine conduit of holy dynamite.

You have the power of the Holy Spirit from which you rule, maintain, and exert dominion. You have the power to step into your home and make it a place that serves the Lord. You have the power to step into your workplace and work as unto the Lord. You have the power to step into your community, town, or city and declare it as part of God's Kingdom.

Finally, the third expression of power Paul referenced is *exusia*. Think of *exusia* as the impact and influence of your power source. If *dunamis* is the source itself, and *kratos* is the focused expression of the source's power, then *exusia* reflects the extent of the power source's reach. *Exusia* is the covering of the Holy Spirit you have because you are saved.

Every unsaved human being remains under the spiritual influence and authority of the devil, the prince of this world.

As for you, you were dead in your transgressions and sins, in which you used to live when you followed the ways of this world and of the ruler of the kingdom of the air, the spirit who is now at work in those who are disobedient.

Ephesians 2:1–2

When you are born again, the devil's influence over you no longer holds sway. Your heavenly Father "enabled you to share in the inheritance that belongs to his people, who live in the light. For he has rescued us from the kingdom of darkness and transferred us into the Kingdom of his dear Son, who purchased our freedom and forgave our sins" (Colossians 1:12–14 NLT).

Because you have the same Spirit within you that raised Christ from the dead, you are no longer subject to Satan's powers. You are able to extend *exusia* power to defeat the enemy and his assaults. Jesus said, "I give unto you power [*exusia*] to tread on serpents and scorpions, and over all the power of the enemy: and nothing shall by any means hurt you" (Luke 10:19 KJV). No matter what we may call it—sin, addiction, despair, defeat, sickness, poverty, or whatever demon crosses our path—we have been given the *exusia* power to defeat it *in the name of Jesus*!

Exponential Power

I realize this is a lot of power to take in—a lot of power! But understanding the distinct aspects of the divine power you possess because of the same Spirit dwelling in you helps you know what you have. Recognizing your ability to access the fullness of your power through the Spirit allows you to multiply your gifts, harvest your blessings, overcome your obstacles, and conquer anything the enemy throws at you.

Do you want more of this power?

Do you desire more of this power?

Do you hunger for more of this power?

Do you need more of this power in your life?

Because of what Jesus did on the cross for you, you have the Holy Spirit in you. Because you have the same Spirit in you, you have direct access to holy dynamite.

Before you were born again, your power was limited to your own. Worse, you were subject to the enemy, the prince of the powers of the air, and his schemes of lies and deceptions against you. But no longer! Now you not only have *dunamis* power within you but can ignite it and express it. You are in a unique position to be both connected to God's power and filled by it. To be charged by it and a conduit of it.

Your relationship with the Holy Spirit would have been different if you had lived before Jesus came and lived on earth. Prior to His birth as a baby in a manger in Bethlehem, the Holy Spirit provided seasons of temporary relationship between humans and God. In the Old Testament, we see how the Spirit of God would descend on individuals—such as King Saul—and then depart. God's Spirit visited people but did not inhabit them. Basically, the Spirit's presence was an extended visitation.

You are in a unique position to be both connected to God's power and filled by it.

But the moment Jesus shed His blood on the cross and paid the price for the forgiveness of all our sins, the Spirit prepared to reside in those who accept the gift of salvation provided through Christ's atonement. The moment Jesus rose from the dead, breathed with new life, and walked out of the tomb, the Spirit became an imminent gift, one delivered at Pentecost so that all believers might have direct relationship with the living God. No more visitations, but permanent dwelling, residing, and inhabiting.

Now that you have the same Spirit within you, your spiritual power extends as you ignite and unleash His power in your life. You experience a fresh anointing, another filling, a recharging of your *kratos* power from your *dunamis* power all under the covering of *exusia* power. Just because the Holy Spirit will never leave you does not mean that you are accessing the fullness of God's power available to you.

Think of it this way. If I poured a pitcher of water over you, you'd get soaked. If you stood in front of a large fan or leaf blower, the water absorbed by your hair, skin, and clothes would dry up pretty quickly. This is the way the Spirit visited people temporarily before Christ came.

But what if I handed you a pitcher of water that you drank? All the water would be inside you. No matter how many fans or leaf blowers you encounter, that water is still with you. This is the gift of the Spirit metabolized within us because of the power of the cross.

Now, though, what if you drank the pitcher of water I gave you and then another was poured over you? You would both have water within you and be saturated in it, demonstrating what happens when you are filled with the Holy Spirit on a fresh anointing. This exponential spiritual power, my friend, is the devil's worst nightmare. Holy Ghost people are connected to *dunamis* power and are freshly charged with the force of its supernatural energy.

Because you are filled with the Spirit, because you have the power of the same Spirit that raised Jesus from the dead sustaining you, then you are no longer bound by your weaknesses, mistakes, struggles, and challenges—you have the power to overcome them all. You can do all things through Christ who strengthens you (see Philippians 4:13). How does He strengthen you? Through His power!

Power Surge

If you've been experiencing a power shortage in your life, then it's time to reignite your wick from the holy fire within you. If you're struggling and desperately afraid you don't have what it takes to keep going, then you need a power surge. If you're feeling trapped by overwhelming circumstances that seem beyond your control, then you need to plug in to your power source and let His holy dynamite make a way where you cannot see one.

God's power parted the Red Sea.

God's power defeated Goliath.

God's power led Ruth to Boaz.

God's power saved Rahab.

God's power brought down the walls of Jericho.

God's power protected Daniel in the lions' den.

God's power turned water into wine.

God's power healed lepers.

God's power turned loaves and fishes into Filet-O-Fish for five thousand.

God's power brought Lazarus back to life.

God's power loves to do the impossible.

And with God, nothing is impossible.

Too often, when we feel as if we're stuck, like we're waiting on God, the truth is that He is waiting on us. He is waiting on us to rely fully on His power—not our own—and to walk by faith and not by sight. I suspect we see some evidence of this when the disciples found their power insufficient—not inadequate—to do what they were asked to do. When they did not get the desired results, Jesus revealed that they had allowed their faith to wane.

When they came to the crowd, a man approached Jesus and knelt before him. "Lord, have mercy on my son," he said. "He has seizures and is suffering greatly. He often falls into the fire or into the water. I brought him to your disciples, but they could not heal him." "You unbelieving and perverse generation," Jesus replied, "how long shall I stay with you? How long shall I put up with you? Bring the boy here to me." Jesus rebuked the demon, and it came out of the boy, and he was healed at that moment. Then the disciples came to Jesus in private and asked, "Why couldn't we drive it out?" He replied, "Because you have so little faith. Truly I tell you, if you have faith as small as a mustard seed, you can say to this mountain, 'Move from here to there,' and it will move. Nothing will be impossible for you."

Matthew 17:14–20

If Jesus' reaction seems harsh at first, I encourage you to consider His disappointment as a sign of the disconnect He observed. He had given His disciples power, and yet the fuel of their faith diminished their connection. Like a faulty electrical wire that interrupts the flow of the current from the source, their efforts lacked connection to the only Source capable of casting out the demon from this boy.

I wonder if we sometimes struggle because we allow our connection to our power source to fray, to unravel, or to get bent out of shape. Rather than seeking a fresh filling of the Spirit, we resort to our own abilities, our own limited human power, and then wonder why we can't keep going, can't blast through, can't see God's miracle being birthed in our mess. In those moments, like the disciples, we must recall that Jesus said we can move mountains with even a tiny mustard grain–sized faith. I wonder if we sometimes struggle because we settle for too little instead of believing for too much.

If your power seems to come and go, to surge sometimes and fade at other times, then it's time to reconnect.

If your power seems to come and go, to surge sometimes and fade at other times, then it's time to reconnect, to recharge in the fullness of the Spirit so that you can move mountains—or what might feel like a mountain in your life right now. A mountain of overwhelming debt. A mountain of recovery from addiction. A mountain of physical therapy after a serious injury. A mountain of honesty and communication after a relational betrayal.

Holy dynamite blasts through those mountains.

Holy dynamite makes a way where you don't see one.

Holy dynamite is in you!

You've Got the Power

You are not where you used to be because you are not who you used to be. The old season cannot handle the new you. The old atmosphere cannot handle the new you. The old drama cannot handle the new you. You may have been born for the past season. But you are born again for the new season!

You have died to sin, and now you are a new creature in Christ. The same Spirit that raised Jesus from the dead—guess what?—*lives in you* (see Romans 8:11). Not just visits. Not just drops in temporarily until the job is done or the miracle performed. No, the same Spirit lives in you, and in Him you live and move and have your being (see Acts 17:28).

If Jesus came out of the tomb, you can come out of anything.

If Jesus came out of the tomb, you can come out of that storm.

If Jesus came out of the tomb, you can come out of addiction.

If Jesus came out of the tomb, you can come out of anxiety.

If Jesus came out of the tomb, you can come out of depression.

If Jesus came out of the tomb, you can come out of generational curses.

If Jesus came out of the tomb, you can come out of failure.

If Jesus came out of the tomb, you can come out of poverty.

If Jesus came out of the tomb, you can come out of rejection.

If Jesus came out of the tomb, you can come out of offense.

If Jesus came out of the tomb, you can come out of the sin.

If Jesus came out of the tomb, you can come out of the past.

Jesus told us, "You will receive *power!*" His power defines us. His power defines you. Spirit-filled people explode with the holy dynamite of God's *dunamis* power.

Holy Spirit people are not weird.

Holy Spirit people are not weak.

Holy Spirit people are not victims.
Holy Spirit people are not whiners.
Holy Spirit people are not beggars.
Holy Spirit people are powerful!

As a matter of fact, the most powerful people on the planet are not those with fame, fortune, or followers. The most powerful people on planet earth are those filled with the Holy Spirit; therefore, let's set the record straight.

Holy Spirit people are wired, not weird.
Holy Spirit people believe and do not beg.
Holy Spirit people are known for their anointing, not for
    disappointing.
Holy Spirit people have power.
Holy Spirit people have *the* power!
Because the Holy Spirit is the greatest empowering force in the
    universe.

His power is unlike any other power and is over every other power. The kind of power that cannot be searched or found on Google, the kind that Amazon Prime does not deliver, that no government stimulus can provide, and that the CDC cannot prescribe.

I'm not talking about just any power. I'm not talking about corrupt, coercive, or controlling power. I'm not talking about temporary, tantalizing, transitional power. I'm talking about *resurrection power*. The same—not similar to or almost like or resembling or next-best-thing—Spirit that raised Jesus Christ out of that tomb lives inside you.

The same Spirit equals *power*.
You can't have the Spirit and be powerless.

You can't have the Spirit and be timid.
You can't have the Spirit and be defeated.
You *have* the Spirit—the same Spirit.
And that changes everything!
Now you praise with power.
Now you pray with power.
Now you preach with power.
Now you live with power.
Now you love with power.
Now you learn with power.
Now you lead with power.
Now you sit with power.
Now you stand with power.
Now you overcome with power.
Now you occupy with power.
You've got the power!
You are full of—and filled with—the power of God!

THE SAME SPIRIT IN YOU

Once again, the questions below are here to assist you in applying this chapter's biblical truths and power-filled promises. They are intended to help you tap deeper into your power source and connect more intimately with God's Spirit. Rather than an obligation or burden, this is an opportunity to refresh yourself in the fullness of the Spirit's power—the same power that resurrected your Savior from death to life. Reflecting on your responses to these questions is beneficial, but you will discover more lasting change if you write down your thoughts so that you can return to them later for further contemplation.

As before, a brief prayer is provided to help focus your time of intimacy with God concerning all you're learning in these pages. Take a deep breath and still yourself before the Lord as you experience His presence within you, around you, beyond you. Remember, you can move mountains because you have holy dynamite.

1. What are some mountains you're struggling to move right now? What have you been waiting on God to do about this mountain? What might He be waiting on you to do?

2. What are your past experiences with being empowered by the Holy Spirit? Has your awareness tended to be based more on what you now understand as *dunamis* power, *kratos* power, or *exusia* power? Why do you think so?

3. What will you do differently today knowing that you have rivers of living water bursting forth from within you? How can you use this power to serve others? To experience more healing in your own life?

—————————————— **PRAYER** ——————————————

Dear Lord, thank You for being my ultimate power source, my holy dynamite that's more forceful than anything I can imagine. Forgive me for the times when I've relied on my own power, when I've allowed my faith to fade and flicker. Rekindle in me a fresh fervor for You and fill me with Your Spirit once again. I know that You reside within me, and so I want to surrender my own attempts to blast through problems and obstacles. Today, I trust You, God, and I know that Your power is sufficient to work through and work in my weakness. I know without a doubt that Your same Spirit of resurrection power is empowering me! In Jesus' name, Amen.

3

EMANCIPATION PROCLAMATION

Breaking Free in the Same Spirit

You cannot have the Holy Spirit and be enslaved.
Where the Spirit of the Lord is present—there is freedom!

When my daughter graduated from high school, our family attended her commencement service. We were excited to see her in her gown and mortarboard walking across the stage and receiving her diploma. The service was held in the auditorium of a large church in our community, a wonderful, Christ-honoring church. Our family arrived early enough to enjoy parking, entering, and finding our seats without rushing into a crowd at the last minute.

With time to spare and our seats selected, I decided to stretch my legs and stroll back to the entrance area of the church. I greeted a few other parents and chatted with a local official I knew. Then, as part of my organizational-management imperative, I began perusing the information available on the table and wall display just inside the front doors. Call it an occupational hazard, but I enjoy reading the literature provided by churches to their guests, visitors, and members.

Usually located in the church lobbies, foyers, and vestibules, as was the case here, such material consists of flyers, handouts, and pamphlets with the intent to inform, invite, and inspire. I never know when an idea or inspiration might strike to use for our own church home. If nothing else, I get to know more about the church I'm visiting, which was my goal while waiting for the commencement exercises to begin.

I picked up what appeared to be the church's general pamphlet of introduction and began to read about this particular body. I enjoyed reading the first paragraph panel and moved on to the second, which sounded much like New Season, the church I am blessed to lead and pastor. Then in the third paragraph panel, I hit a speed bump. No, a brick wall! Within the narrative description of this church's identity, a strong statement jumped out and grasped my undivided attention: *We are not a Pentecostal church.*

Wow!

Such a simple statement, yet so revealing.

They wanted to be sure that no one mistook them for a Pentecostal church. They do not consider being Pentecostal part of who they are or what they are about. Okay, got it.

I experienced a plethora of emotions colliding at once: disappointment, hurt, concern, compassion, conviction. After I momentarily considered the idea of speaking in tongues loudly to activate security, I acquiesced and embraced a more mature posture befitting a believer, a pastor, and the proud father of a graduate that day.

Nonetheless, I had to question why. What motivated this church to define itself by what it is not? What had they seen in Pentecostal people to prompt this stand? Or, perhaps, what were they afraid might happen if they were a Pentecostal church? Maybe they simply didn't understand true Pentecostalism.

While I returned to my seat and enjoyed celebrating my daughter's milestone achievement, I was haunted by that six-word sentence.

We are not a Pentecostal church. I was also convicted to make sure the following Sunday when I stood in the pulpit before my congregation to make my own six-word proclamation: We *are*, indeed, a Pentecostal church!

With great due deference to my brothers and sisters in that other church, I wanted to be clear that in our house, we are not ashamed to say that we are a prophetic church. We are a Spirit-friendly community of believers. We are a Holy Ghost–empowered congregation. And we believe in miracles, signs, and wonders.

Within our body, we speak English, Spanish, Romanian, Russian, French, Italian, Vietnamese, and Mandarin, and many of us speak and have a prayer language. We believe there's an anointing for the assignment God calls us to fulfill. We believe the young will have visions and the old will have dreams.

We believe the Holy Spirit came down so that we can get up; therefore, with great deference, respect, and Christian love, I was thrilled to declare that from the top of our heads to the bottoms of our feet, we are a church born on Pentecost.

Trailer for Truth

One of my gravest concerns about the sentence in the pamphlet from the other church is the message it sends to people seeking God. I never want to disburse any communication, personally or on behalf of the Church and believers worldwide, that conveys exclusion, restrictions, and "no vacancy." There was no room at the inn for Mary and Joseph to bring baby Jesus into this world, but my hope is that there is always room for everyone in God's Church.

More and more, I encounter people who are hungry for the Spirit of God. I run into men and women who are starving for authentic spiritual power, who are sick and tired of floundering within their own limitations, and who are suffering from attacks by dark forces. Whether they have hit rock bottom or scaled the heights of success, they come to me seeking God and wanting to experience His power.

In fact, I was in Hollywood recently when a producer came to me after a meeting and asked, "Is your church a Holy Spirit church?"

We locked eyes, and I smiled. "*Yes*! I can promise you that our church is a Holy Spirit church!"

"Good," he said, appearing relieved. "That's what I want. Because I don't just know God is real—I feel it. And I want to feel Him even more!"

We are people of the Spirit, the same Spirit that raised Jesus from the dead.

We are Holy Spirit–led people of the head, heart, and hand, with heads full of conviction informed by the Spirit, hearts full of compassion inspired by the Spirit, and hands full of charitable acts imparted by the Spirit—we know it, we feel it, we live it.

My friend the producer's question reminded me that God's Spirit advertises the Lord's goodness and power through us. Yes, an advertisement unlike any commercial on TV, pop-up on a website, billboard in Times Square, glossy page in a magazine, banner pulled behind a plane, or email blast. Your life is a trailer for truth! Remember Paul's prayer for the believers in Ephesus? "I pray that you will continually experience the immeasurable greatness of God's power made available to you through faith. Then your lives will be an advertisement of this immense power as it works through you!" (Ephesians 1:19 TPT).

The same Spirit that made you lives inside of you.

As God's immense power works through us, our lives become living advertisements of His dynamic, explosive, unlimited *dunamis* power at work. When holy dynamite ignites within us, others notice. How could they not see a difference in our lives?

The same Spirit that made you lives inside of you. The architect is now the tenant. What is the Holy Spirit's permanent address? *You*!

God's Word confirms His residence within you. "The Spirit of God has made me; the breath of the Almighty gives me life" (Job 33:4). Paul asked, "Don't you know that you yourselves are God's temple and that God's Spirit dwells in your midst?" (1 Corinthians 3:16).

Where can someone find the Spirit? Wherever they find you! Where can your friends, family, frenemies, and followers find Him when they are in need? Wherever they find you! You are a living, breathing, walking, and talking advertisement for the Spirit in you.

In your words.

In your look.

In your touch.

In your posts.

In your actions.

In your atmosphere.

In your prayers.

In your praise.

In your faith.

In your values.

You are advertising the same Spirit that raised Jesus from the dead.

Your Spiritual Birthright

Others see in you what you experience in the power of God's Spirit. With God's *dunamis* power inside you, you cannot be powerless—it's impossible. Once anointed with fresh oil, Holy Spirit people are the most powerful people on the planet because the same Spirit that raised Jesus from death to life is the source of your power. If the Holy Spirit brought your Savior out of the tomb, He can bring you out of anything.

When you're in a tomb, the Spirit has a plan to bring you back to life. When you're in a prison, the Spirit has the power to unlock your cell. When you're in a corner, the Spirit makes a way where there was a wall.

Using God's power to liberate you is another glorious blessing of the Holy Spirit within you. "Now the Lord is the Spirit, and where the Spirit of the Lord is, there is freedom" (2 Corinthians 3:17 ESV). This eternal, biblical truth is about God's precious Spirit—both who He is and what He does.

For clarity, consider the way this verse, which is more than worthy of memorization and meditation, is rendered in a different translation: "Now, the 'Lord' I'm referring to is the Holy Spirit, and wherever he is Lord, there is freedom" (2 Corinthians 3:17 TPT). Where the Holy Spirit is Lord, there is freedom. Where is the Holy Spirit? In you; therefore, freedom is in you as well.

What kind of freedom are we talking about? I'm glad you asked. The most important, essential, vital freedom in existence—your spiritual freedom. Holy Spirit freedom.

In order to understand the unique distinction of Holy Spirit freedom, we must start by considering freedom in general. According to the Merriam-Webster online dictionary, *freedom* is defined as "the quality or state of being free, such as: the absence of necessity, coercion, or constraint in choice or action; liberation from slavery or from the power of another."[1] Other synonyms for *freedom* include *independence*, *liberty*, *autonomy*, and *being unrestricted*. The opposite of freedom is captivity, oppression, or bondage.

Just to clarify further, the freedom in the Holy Spirit I'm talking about does not come from ancient philosophies based on the Egyptians, the Greeks, or the Romans. The freedom that we have did not come when King John signed the Magna Carta in 1215.

The freedom that we have does not come from our Founding Fathers or their vision for our government. Our freedom does not come from George Washington, John Adams, Thomas Jefferson, James Madison, or James Monroe.

The freedom that we have comes from the most transformative, powerful force on the planet—the Holy Spirit of God!

Totalitarian, authoritarian, communist, and socialist governments fear Bible-believing Christians more than they fear any military force or political ideology on earth. Why? Simply stated, because of the power it has to set people free. Inherent in its power, the Gospel of Jesus sets people free. "So if the Son sets you free, you will be free indeed" (John 8:36 ESV).

Freedom is power.

Freedom and faith destroy fear.

Freedom has no bars, walls, chains, or locks.

Once you're freed by the Spirit, you will never be spiritually incarcerated again. "For freedom Christ has set us free; stand firm therefore, and do not submit again to a yoke of slavery" (Galatians 5:1 ESV).

Once you're freed by the Spirit, you use your freedom to free others. "For you were called to freedom, brothers. Only do not use your freedom as an opportunity for the flesh, but through love serve one another" (Galatians 5:13 ESV).

Once you're freed by the Spirit, your life is never the same. "Live as people who are free, not using your freedom as a cover-up for evil, but living as servants of God" (1 Peter 2:16 ESV).

Once you're freed by the Spirit, you see clearly and cannot be deceived by the enemy. "You will know the truth, and the truth will set you free" (John 8:32 ESV).

When you're born again, freedom is your spiritual birthright.

The Holy Spirit is freedom, and the same Spirit is in you. When you're born again, freedom is your spiritual birthright.

Lifting Your Veil

You cannot have the Holy Spirit and be enslaved.

Where the Spirit of the Lord is present—there is freedom!

When Jesus died on the cross and rose from the grave, your freedom was secured in a way previously unknown. Just as the Holy Spirit was a temporary visitor to those who knew God before these history-altering, life-transforming events, their freedom was limited as well. Paul offers us a before-and-after glimpse of freedom in his second letter to believers at Corinth. He made it clear that our confidence in being free comes from "our great trust in God through Christ" (2 Corinthians 3:4 NLT), not because of any action or qualification of our own.

Instead, we are now qualified for eternal freedom because we're ministers of the new covenant relationship established through the Holy Spirit. Paul explained, "This is a covenant not of written laws, but of the Spirit. The old written covenant ends in death; but under the new covenant, the Spirit gives life" (2 Corinthians 3:6 NLT).

The old covenant with God's people relied on their adherence to the law established by, but not limited to, the Ten Commandments, which God gave to Moses on Mount Sinai. When Moses returned to deliver God's Ten Commandments carved into stone tablets, people were unable to look at him.

> The old way, with laws etched in stone, led to death, though it began with such glory that the people of Israel could not bear to look at Moses' face. For his face shone with the glory of God, even though the brightness was already fading away. Shouldn't we expect far greater glory under the new way, now that the Holy Spirit is giving life? If the old way, which brings condemnation, was glorious, how much more glorious is the new way, which makes us right with God! In fact, that first glory was not glorious at all compared with the overwhelming glory of the new way. So if the old way, which has been replaced, was glorious, how much more glorious is the new, which remains forever!
>
> 2 Corinthians 3:7–11 NLT

The old way was glorious enough at the time because it enabled people to know God prior to Jesus' birth, death, and resurrection. But since Jesus came, paid the price for our sins, and triumphed over death, He created a new way—even more glorious because of its permanence. This new freedom in the Spirit means that nothing separates us from God. We no longer have to avert our gaze from the glory of the Lord because His glory resides in us. Paul emphasized this difference now that the veil of the old way is no longer required.

> But whenever someone turns to the Lord, the veil is taken away. For the Lord is the Spirit, and wherever the Spirit of the Lord is, there is freedom. So all of us who have had that veil removed can see and reflect the glory of the Lord. And the Lord—who is the Spirit—makes us more and more like him as we are changed into his glorious image.
>
> 2 Corinthians 3:16–18 NLT

In this passage we see how context illuminates our understanding of the freedom we have in the Spirit. When we isolate a Scripture verse without analyzing the surrounding verses, we risk misunderstanding, diluting, or losing its full meaning. To understand the context is liberating. This is what we find here, literally and figuratively, with Paul's comparison and contrast of the old way based on the law with the new way reliant on the Spirit. Basically, Paul exposes the illusion of freedom exhibited by Moses and those following the law. It was illusory because it was conditional on their obedience, which was never consistent and never enough.

Keep in mind, too, that Paul wrote this while filled with God's Holy Spirit. Ultimately, God wants us to see that the illusion of freedom cannot compare to the absolute freedom we have now in Christ. Moses wore a veil in order to hide the fact that the glory he experienced in his conversations with God was temporary and would fade away. Moses was bound to the law; therefore, the glory was temporary.

Now that we can have the Holy Spirit in us, we are free—completely and eternally—and no longer need the veil. In other words, Moses had an illusion of freedom through the law, but you and I have the reality of freedom through the Holy Spirit. The Spirit has the power to accomplish what the law could never accomplish: a personal relationship with God through the atoning work of Christ in which the glory will never fade. Paul wanted believers to know that where the Spirit of the Lord is, there is freedom from glory to glory.

This means that you no longer need a veil, a stone tablet, or the old way. This means that you fix your eyes on Jesus directly, have the same Spirit within you, and know the new way.

Consequently, you need to know that you're not going to go from problem to problem, from pandemic to pandemic, from fear to failure, from anxiety to depression, from shame to condemnation, from unforgiveness to unbelief, from debt to despair, or from drama to disillusionment.

Quite the opposite.

Are you ready to be free?

You and your house—because you are free by the Holy Spirit—are about to go from blessed to favor, from survive to thrive, from enough to more than enough, from living to abundant living, from occupying to owning, from hearing about Jesus, reading about Jesus, learning about Jesus, and worshiping Jesus to forgiving like Jesus, loving like Jesus, and healing like Jesus. "And we all, with unveiled face, beholding the glory of the Lord, are being transformed into the same image from one degree of glory to another. For this comes from the Lord who is the Spirit" (2 Corinthians 3:18 ESV).

Freedom is the bridge from one level of glory to the next.

Lift your veil, my friend.

Unlock Your Limitations

When you have lifted the veil and experienced the glory of God's Spirit dwelling in you, empowering you, and befriending you, then freedom takes on a whole new meaning. Experiencing your freedom is proof of the Holy Spirit's presence in your life—all areas, dimensions, situations, relationships, nooks, and crannies of your existence. Maybe you know this is true theologically but still struggle to grasp it deeply, personally, intimately. Perhaps you want more evidence, more clarity, more personal application.

How do you know the Holy Spirit is present?
How do you know the Holy Spirit is in your life?
How do you know the Holy Spirit is in your family?
How do you know the Holy Spirit is in your church?

Before we answer these questions, consider what enslaves you or what might be clouding your understanding of the freedom you have in the Spirit.

What has you locked up in overwhelming fear?
What has you chained to insurmountable pain?
What has you imprisoned in unbearable shame?
What has you incarcerated with debilitating despair?
Because you can't be shackled to the old way anymore.
You can't hide behind your veil and look away.
You can't have both the Holy Spirit and captivity.
You can't have both the Holy Spirit and bondage.
You can't have both the Holy Spirit and slavery.
Because where the Holy Spirit is present, there is no veil.
Where the Holy Spirit is present, there is no captivity.
Where the Holy Spirit is present, there is no bondage.
Where the Holy Spirit is present, there is no slavery.

When the Holy Spirit is present, when the Holy Spirit occupies a space, when the Holy Spirit inhabits a person or a place, then there *must* be *freedom*! Freedom from and freedom to . . .

Freedom from sin.
Freedom from shame.
Freedom from anxiety.
Freedom from addiction.
Freedom from fear.

Freedom from failure.

Freedom from depression.

Freedom from oppression.

Freedom from generational curses.

Freedom from living in a lie.

Freedom from living with a lid.

Freedom from troubling thoughts.

Freedom from negative thinking.

Freedom from unbelief.

Freedom from unforgiveness.

You are free, my friend, so you can no longer live as one enslaved! "At last we have freedom, for Christ has set us free! We must always cherish this truth and firmly refuse to go back into the bondage of our past" (Galatians 5:1 TPT). Where the Spirit of the Lord is present, not only are we free from, but we have . . .

Freedom to live holy.

Freedom to pursue righteousness.

Freedom to grow in God's Word.

Freedom to occupy the blessings.

Freedom to possess the promise.

Freedom to go from glory to glory.

Freedom to remove the veil.

Freedom to worship.

Freedom to praise.

Freedom to pray.

Freedom to lay hands on the sick.

Freedom to cast out devils.

Freedom to speak truth with love.

Freedom to exercise the gifts.

Freedom to transfer the mantle to the next generation.

Your freedom means that you can no longer live the way you once lived, behind a veil and locked into your own limitations. The Holy Spirit has ripped away your veil and your limitations.

Don't stand around wondering how you can be free when the chains are broken, the door is open, and the walls have come crumbling down.

> Beloved ones, God has called us to live a life of freedom. But don't view this wonderful freedom as an excuse to set up a base of operations in the natural realm. Constantly love each other and be committed to serve one another.
>
> Galatians 5:13 TPT

Free People Free People

The Spirit of Jesus sets people—people just like you and me—free. Wherever the Spirit of the Lord is, there is freedom. The Spirit of the Lord is in you and in me. Holy Spirit people are free people. Free from everything that has tried to encumber you, to hold you, to bear down on you, to crush you, to overwhelm you. No more!

Your freedom is power. Your freedom sends fear running. Your freedom has no walls. Yes, Holy Spirit people are free. And free people—they free people!

The most powerful human on the planet is a person set free by the Spirit of the living God. Why? Because free people can do what others cannot.

It was a free man who approached Pharaoh in Egypt and said, "Let my people go" (Exodus 9:1).

It was a free man who stepped into the Promised Land and declared, "As for me and my household, we will serve the LORD" (Joshua 24:15).

It was a free man in his eighties who lifted his voice and said, "Give me my mountain" (see Joshua 14:12).

It was a free man who stepped out of the winepress that he was using as a threshing floor to free his people from the Midianite marauders when heaven freed him by reminding him of his true identity, that of a mighty warrior (see Judges 7, 8).

It was a free man who stared down a giant called Goliath and said, "You come against me with sword and spear and javelin, but I come against you in the name of the LORD Almighty, the God of the armies of Israel" (1 Samuel 17:45).

It was a free group of young people who refused to bow and subsequently exhibited freedom even in the midst of a fiery furnace (see Daniel 3:16–22).

It was a free man who prayed down fire from heaven and then shouted, "Get ready. Here comes the rain" (see 1 Kings 18:44).

It was a free man who opened his mouth and said, "I can't stay quiet, I must prophesy. It is just like fire shut up in my bones" (see Jeremiah 20:9).

It was a free woman who said, "Your people will be my people and your God my God" (Ruth 1:16).

It was a free woman who said, "If I only touch his cloak, I will be healed" (Matthew 9:21).

It was a free woman who said, "Even the dogs eat the crumbs that fall from their master's table" (Matthew 15:27).

In more recent history, it was a group of free men who declared, "We hold these truths to be self-evident, that all men are created equal, that they are endowed by their Creator with certain unalienable Rights, that among these are Life, Liberty and the pursuit of Happiness."

It was a free man who confronted the evils of slavery, proclaimed emancipation for all people, and then declared, "With malice toward none with charity for all."[2]

It was a free man who had a dream that one day we would live in a nation where we are not judged by the color of our skin but rather the content of our character.[3]

But the greatest expression of freedom in all of time and beyond came some two thousand years ago when, hanging on a tree by His sacrifice, Jesus Christ, a free man and freedom incarnate, embodied the ultimate emancipation proclamation. "So if the Son sets you free, you will be free indeed" (John 8:36 ESV).

For eternal freedom, freedom of the soul, freedom of the spirit, and freedom to go beyond existence to living does not come from the institutions or writings of human beings. Our freedom comes from He who wrote the law with one finger and grace with both hands. Our freedom comes from the Great Liberator and Lover of our souls.

Our freedom is contagious and frees others!

Let Freedom Ring

Living in freedom carries repercussions.

One of our country's patriotic treasures is the Liberty Bell, proudly displayed in the City of Brotherly Love, Philadelphia, in my home state of Pennsylvania. While it has that famous crack silencing its clapper, the ideals it embodies continue to resonate. But *our* symbol of liberty echoes with the power of God's Spirit. Through the power of the cross, our freedom rings loud and clear and can never be silenced. Through the power of the Gospel, our freedom rings true with great news.

The great news is that through Jesus Christ you can be free from a life of sin (see Revelation 1:5).

The great news is that you now know the truth, and it shall set you free (see John 8:32).

The great news is that in Christ you can be free from the torment of fear (see 2 Timothy 1:7).

The great news is that in Christ you can be free from the sentence of eternal condemnation (see Romans 8:1).

The great news is that when you know His freedom, your life can never be the same because you are a new creature in Christ (see 2 Corinthians 5:17).

Free people live differently, look differently, and love differently. Free people are baptized with Christ in Romans, crucified with Christ in Galatians, seated with Christ in Ephesians, strengthened by Christ in Philippians, hidden in Christ in Colossians, and reign with Christ in Revelation. Behold the Lamb!

Free people can't be silenced.
Free people can't be trampled on.
Free people can't be placed in a corner.
Free people can't be defeated.
Free people can't go back to the old way.
What do free people do?
Free people sing, worship, gather, love, give, serve, and prophesy.
Free people change the world!

If you have not been living in the fullness of your freedom, it's time to redeem the narrative. Your story is not what it used to be. Your Savior has authored new chapters more glorious than what you can imagine.

Once an addict, always an addict?
Once Jesus sets you free, you are free indeed.
Once injured, always crippled?
Once Jesus sets you free, you are free indeed.
Once an adulterer, always an adulterer?
Once Jesus sets you free, you are free indeed.
Once a thief, always a thief?
Once Jesus sets you free, you are free indeed.

No matter what you thought you were or would always be, your script has been flipped.

You are free to be who God created you to be!

Have your questions been answered? Do you know what freedom is? Better still, are you free?

Are you truly free?

People on probation with an ankle bracelet may look free, act free, and dress free, but the moment they cross a certain line they discover that freedom is an illusion. They are still bound to the consequences of what they've done. Their mobility is still limited by the punishment of their crime.

God wants to set you free from the illusion of freedom. Free from the "bracelet" of religious coercion. Free from secular intimidation. Free from generational manipulation. Free from self-mutilation.

Remove the veil. Remove the illusion. No more fading glory. You are free forevermore in the same Spirit.

Let your freedom ring!

THE SAME SPIRIT IN YOU

By now you know that the questions below are offered to help you process and apply the truths of God's Word explored in this chapter. You're encouraged to read them slowly and to think through them carefully, inviting the Holy Spirit within you to whisper what you need to focus on. Consider those areas where you have continued living as if you were bound by the old life you knew before Jesus set you free. Reflect on the next steps you need to take in order to experience the fullness of living in the freedom of the Spirit.

Once again, the brief prayer below is provided to begin your communication with God about all you're thinking, feeling, learning, and experiencing as you've been reading and processing. Before you begin, take a moment and still your heart in His presence, listening for His voice, the familiar voice of your Good Shepherd, who knows and loves you. Ask Him to show you where you continue to veil yourself from the glorious gift of His freedom in your life.

1. When you consider that your life is an advertisement for the power of God's Spirit in you, what do you suppose others see? What do you hope they can see?

2. How would you describe the distinction Paul makes in Corinthians between the old way of experiencing spiritual freedom from sin and the new way provided by Jesus on the cross?

3. What are some ways you continue to veil yourself from the reality of your freedom in Christ? What's holding you back from exercising the power of freedom within you?

———————————— PRAYER ————————————

Dear God, forgive me for the times I've said I wanted to experience freedom from my sins, my struggles, and my addictions while still relying on my own efforts behind a veil of pride. I know that You are the only source of my freedom, Your Spirit dwelling in me and filling me with Your miraculous, healing power. I pray that You would shine through me, Lord, allowing my life to advertise Your power and Your freedom to those around me. Thank You that I am free in Christ to be the person You have created me to be. In Jesus' name, Amen.

4

BILINGUAL BENEFITS

Speaking in the Same Spirit

When you are filled with the Holy Spirit, you speak what you have never spoken before!
You are now fluent in a language of holiness, freedom, and power!

I grew up in a bilingual home where we spoke both Spanish and English. My parents had migrated from Puerto Rico to Pennsylvania, so Spanish was their native language; however, they insisted on their children learning to speak English. I remain grateful to them for recognizing the advantages of being bilingual, honoring the rich historical and cultural language of their homeland while also embracing the common communication of their new home. Perhaps my mother and father also saw a future in which Spanish would grow in usage across our country.

Like most children, I learned language by absorbing the Spanish spoken most often around me. To be more precise, we spoke Puerto Rican Spanish, a dialect with its own unique characteristics and idiosyncrasies. As a kid, of course, I didn't realize that my ancestral native language was not the same as that of Spanish speakers around the world. It was simply the language I learned, which included things like replacing the *R* sound at the end of some syllables with an *L* sound. And rather than rolling our double *R*s in a word the usual Spanish way, our double *R*s sounded like a guttural *H*. Without realizing why or how, I learned the unvoiced pronunciation of certain syllables and how to aspirate the *S* at the end of others. I didn't think about the linguistic formalities or cultural quirks at the time—I just wanted to employ the primary function of language, communication.

As an adult, I've appreciated the mental dexterity required to speak, read, and comprehend two languages simultaneously. When I preach, depending on those present, I feel the freedom to switch from English to Spanish and back again, to benefit from when one language more aptly or accurately expresses my intended message. This duality has not only benefited my cultural, educational, and professional communication skills but also enhanced my brain's neurological functioning.

According to neuroscientist Dr. John Grundy, a professor at Iowa State University who specializes in bilingualism, learning a new language creates new neural pathways, resulting in enhanced neuroplasticity in the brain. As a person becomes more fluent in an additional language, the process shifts from their brain's frontal lobes to parts focused on "more automatic motor processing and automatic sensory information."[1]

This shift makes the language easier and more natural to its speaker, which is the linguistic dexterity I experience thanks to being bilingual at an early age. "It's really just a remodeling of the brain that allows it to become more efficient," explains Dr. Grundy.[2] Once new language functioning shifts into automatic, speed and facility increase because the speaker no longer has to think about translating from one to another.

While there are approximately 76 million bilingual speakers in the United States right now, roughly a quarter of the 330 million-plus inhabitants, it's never too late to learn a new language and experience the benefits.[3] In fact, according to numerous experts like Dr. Grundy, learning a second language helps to prevent, or at least delay, cognitive decline as we age. "There is a consistent finding that bilinguals are able to stave off symptoms of dementia for about four to six years compared to monolinguals."[4]

With all due respect to these insightful benefits, there is another language with *unlimited* benefits for those of us who know Jesus Christ—the language of the Holy Spirit.

Divine Dialect

I was fortunate to learn both Spanish and English at home, with my American English fluency greatly supplemented by my reading and writing classes at school, not to mention being surrounded by mostly English-speaking students, peers, and teachers. This made learning both languages easier because each was used contextually—one at home and one at school—while still overlapping at times. Many experts believe children absorb languages more easily because their brains are still developing and have plenty of capacity before years of new data and life experience get processed.

As an adult, I've also dabbled in learning to speak additional languages. Recently my wife and I were planning a trip to Italy, so a few months prior to our planned visit, she surprised me with the gift of an online course in Italian from Rosetta Stone, a renowned leader in language learning thanks to its proprietary software programs. I confess that I did not make full use of the resources available with this online program, but I benefited, nonetheless.

There are certainly plenty of other options when trying to learn a new language, including in-person classroom instruction, private tutoring, online conversation partners, and immersive experiences in a community of native speakers. If you have capacity or fluency in a language other than English, reflect for a moment on how you learned it. Was your language learning influenced more by studying vocabulary and grammar, or by interacting directly with proficient speakers on a regular basis?

Regardless of your linguistic education in the past, you have a bilingual ability you may not be using. If you have been born again in the Spirit and accepted the free gift of salvation through the sacrifice of Jesus on the cross and the power of His resurrection, then you are already fluent in the divine dialect of faith. Fresh oil anoints your capacity for divine communication. The language of the Holy Spirit makes you a native speaker of your true homeland—heaven. "For this world is not our home; we are looking forward to our everlasting home in heaven" (Hebrews 13:14 TLB).

When you are filled with the Spirit of God, the first sign you see is that you speak what you have never spoken before. This fact is not based on my opinion, observation, or personal experience. This fact is based on God's Word and the record it provides of what occurred at the Festival of Pentecost following the death and resurrection of Christ. You will recall that just prior to His ascension into heaven, Jesus told His disciples to get ready because "you will receive power when the Holy Spirit comes upon you. And you will be my witnesses, telling people about me everywhere—in Jerusalem, throughout Judea, in Samaria, and to the ends of the earth" (Acts 1:8 NLT).

You are fluent in the divine language of faith.

You will also recall that the disciples were eager to know when they could expect to receive this divine power their Master promised, to which Jesus replied that only the Father knows (see Acts 1:7). So how long did they have to wait before they unwrapped the gift of the Holy Spirit? Based on the events referenced, we know that ten days passed from when Jesus ascended into the clouds before their eyes to when they all gathered together for the Jewish celebration known as the Feast of Pentecost, which was also called the Harvest Feast.

Jesus died during the Feast of Passover and then spent forty days interacting with His followers after His resurrection. In the Jewish calendar of holy days, Pentecost occurred fifty days after Passover, which means for ten days, the followers of Jesus waited. I'll speculate that those were ten of the longest days these disciples had experienced. They knew Jesus would keep His promise to them. After all, He had foretold His death and resurrection, both of which had come to pass. So they knew something big—whatever this gift of the Holy Spirit was all about—was about to go down. Which meant they couldn't just resume their everyday routines and get on with life. They had to wait. To wait expectantly. To wait patiently. To wait faithfully.

Have you ever had to wait on something you knew was coming even though you didn't know exactly when it would arrive? Enduring those seasons can be excruciating. It is hard living in the tension of knowing, expecting, and waiting while also being uncertain, impatient, and perhaps doubtful. You know it's going to happen, but what if something goes wrong?

We wait on babies to arrive, on marriage proposals to be made, on promotions to come through. We wait on degrees to be conferred, on test results to come back negative, on wounds to heal. We wait on friends to arrive, on conflicts to be resolved, on hard conversations to be spoken.

But what those early believers waited on carried even more expectation and uncertainty! And what they experienced was unlike any gift in the history of the world, before or after.

Making an Entrance

So the disciples waited and they waited and they waited. For more than a week, they waited to see what would happen. Perhaps some wondered if they would know this gift right away when they saw it. Or whether it might sneak up on them in such a subtle, discreet way that they wouldn't be sure of its arrival.

Having waited for ten days, they gathered for the annual Jewish celebration of Pentecost. The observance of this holy day was closely linked to Passover, the weeklong commemoration of God's deliverance of the people of Israel from bondage in Egypt. Through His chosen leader, Moses, God had instructed the Jewish people to make a specific sacrifice a certain way and to place blood from this sacrifice on their doorposts in the evening. The Lord told them:

> On that same night I will pass through Egypt and strike down every firstborn of both people and animals, and I will bring judgment on all the gods of Egypt. I am the LORD. The blood will be a sign for you on the houses where you are, and when I see the blood, I will pass over you. No destructive plague will touch you when I strike Egypt.
>
> Exodus 12:12–13

The Israelites were instructed at the same time to commemorate that event "for the generations to come . . . as a festival to the LORD—a lasting ordinance" (verse 14). Numerous instructions were also provided for the time following Passover, including the Feast of Weeks, observed seven weeks and one day later—fifty days. In fact, because this feast was held fifty days after Passover, it became known as Pentecost, from the Greek word for fiftieth.

Just as Passover commemorated God's deliverance of His people, Pentecost celebrated God's provision for His people. Following their exodus from Egypt, the Israelites searched for the Promised Land for forty years. During that time, they learned to rely on God to meet their needs, particularly for water and bread, or manna, as the flaky substance was called. Consequently, Pentecost required offerings from that year's wheat harvest, including two loaves of bread (see Exodus 34:22; Leviticus 23:15–17).

You might be thinking, "Great history lesson, Pastor Sam, but what does this have to do with the Holy Spirit?" Everything, my friend! Once again, context reveals that with God, there is no such thing as coincidence. While the disciples waited those ten days after Christ's ascension not knowing when they would receive their gift, we see in historical hindsight that the Feast of Pentecost beautifully symbolizes God's new provision to His people just as Jesus became the Lamb of God sacrificed fifty days prior at Passover.

So, it seems totally logical for the gift of the Holy Spirit to be delivered to believers on Pentecost, historically a Jewish holy day celebrating the Lord's provisions, bounty, and abundance to the people of Israel following their deliverance from Egypt. The birth, death, and resurrection of Jesus changed everything, and Pentecost was no exception.

Instead of commemorating what God had done for them—past tense—these believers received the timeless gift of God's Spirit in the present moment, the same Spirit that dwells in you and me. And there was no mistaking the arrival of the Spirit and His immediate impact on their lives:

> On the day of Pentecost all the believers were meeting together in one place. Suddenly, there was a sound from heaven like the roaring of a mighty windstorm, and it filled the house where they were sitting. Then, what looked like flames or tongues of fire appeared and settled on each of them. And everyone present was filled with the Holy Spirit and began speaking in other languages, as the Holy Spirit gave them this ability.
>
> Acts 2:1–4 NLT

Talk about being unmistakably from the Lord. Now that's the way to make an unforgettable entrance!

What Went Down in the Upper Room

On the Day of Pentecost almost two thousand years ago, a group of 120 believers in Jesus Christ gathered together to receive the power of the Holy Spirit that their Master had promised them (see Acts 1:8). And the room where this group gathered and received the Spirit of God with a mighty wind and tongues of fire was no random, arbitrary place. The Holy Spirit came down in the Upper Room.

This venue was the same Upper Room were Jesus and His disciples had their last meal together prior to Christ's arrest and crucifixion. Jesus gave instructions on where they were to go and who they were to talk with in order to find a place for them to observe their Passover meal together. "Then he [the master of the house] will show you a large, furnished upper room; there make ready" (Luke 22:12 NKJV).

And this Passover observance together was not just the typical Jewish Seder meal—it was the Last Supper. And what took place at the Last Supper? Jesus took bread, blessed it, broke it, and gave it to His disciples, saying, "This is My body which is given for you; do this in remembrance of Me" (verse 19 NKJV). Then Jesus took a cup of wine, blessed it, and said, "This cup is the new covenant in My blood, which is shed for you" (verse 20 NKJV).

So, they ate the bread symbolic of Christ's broken body, and they drank wine from the cup symbolic of Christ's blood shed for the forgiveness of our sins.

What happened in the Upper Room? They had fellowship and they had communion. But other things took place in the Upper Room that night.

Jesus exposed Judas's plot to betray Him (see verse 21).

Jesus told Peter that he was going to deny Him three times (see verse 34).

What difference does it make that the room where all these events transpired just fifty days prior became the landing pad for the Holy Spirit to descend on believers? To transform the disciples' understanding of where God meets them to fill them with His power!

The Holy Spirit descended and filled those present in the identical room where Jesus had fellowship and communion in the presence of betrayal and denial. Jesus knew this was the last time His twelve disciples would all be with Him. Jesus knew full well what Judas had already done and would do next. Jesus knew that Peter, so passionate and yet so afraid, would deny even knowing Him. Jesus knew that the bread and wine they shared would set the sacramental precedent for Communion that believers would share until He returned. That night when so much was going down in the Upper Room, the tension had to be practically palpable.

And yet, that is not what we must remember most about the Upper Room. Because when the Holy Spirit descended, that place became the birthplace for Spirit-filled Christ followers. When the Holy Spirit descended, holy fire was sparked that can never be snuffed out. When the Holy Spirit descended in the Upper Room, God's power was unleashed in the lives of men and women whose lives would never be the same.

The same Spirit blowing through the pain, betrayal, and heartache of their Upper Room now blows through those places in your life. If you know what it means to be betrayed, to be rejected, or to be un-followed, then you know those places I'm talking about. Those tender areas that still have not healed. Those relationships that have drifted apart. Those sites where you lost something—or someone—you didn't believe you could live without.

> When the Holy Spirit descended, holy fire was sparked that can never be snuffed out.

Yet, by the power of the Holy Spirit in you, you now feel a windstorm of healing blowing in. Through the power of the same Spirit in you that descended into believers in that Upper Room, you now know freedom. And with the Spirit of God within you, you now speak a new language of holiness.

Jesus brought fellowship and community to the Upper Room despite the painful betrayals and disappointing denials. And then on Pentecost, the gift He promised transformed that place into the birthplace of the Church.

God never changes. "Jesus Christ is the same yesterday and today and forever" (Hebrews 13:8). What He did then in the Upper Room, He is doing now in your Upper Room. You may have sealed the attic door, boarded over the windows, and told yourself you would never go back into that Upper Room and the painful memories it holds. But thanks be to God, through the power of the same Spirit, you can unlock that door, open those windows, and feel the wind of power, freedom, and peace blowing in a breeze of blessing.

The Holy Spirit continues to fill those places inside you, my friend.

In spite of the Peters who denied you and the Judases who betrayed you, that area, that chapter, that place in your life will not be known for the pain. It will be known for the fulfillment of the promise.

Get ready for the Holy Spirit to fill your area of pain.

Get ready for the Holy Spirit to fill the area where you experienced betrayal.

Get ready for the Holy Spirit to fill the same area where your God-ordained purpose was once denied.

Get ready for the Holy Spirit to fill your Upper Room.

I'm here to tell you the Holy Spirit will give birth to something amazing in the same place where you suffered betrayal and denial. Your Upper Room will be known for the outpouring and anointing you experience there. Pentecost reminds us that the place of denial and betrayal will be the same place of the greatest outpouring.

The same Spirit that filled the Upper Room is about to fill your bedroom and heal your marriage.

The same Spirit that filled the Upper Room is about to fill your living room and heal your family.

The same Spirit that filled the Upper Room is about to fill your basement and restore what's broken and in storage.

The same Spirit that filled the Upper Room is about to fill and heal every room in your house.

We are children of the cross. We are the fruit of the empty tomb. We are the product of the Upper Room!

Wait for Your Suddenly

In Acts 1, Jesus tells his disciples to wait.

In Acts 2, the same disciples experienced a *suddenly*. "Suddenly they heard the sound of a violent blast of wind rushing into the house from out of the heavenly realm. The roar of the wind was so overpowering it was all anyone could bear!" (Acts 2:2 TPT). After waiting those ten days without knowing when, how, or if what was promised would be delivered, the disciples received it suddenly.

We experience a suddenly when we believe that the God of the process is the God of the promise, that the God of eternity is the God of the all-at-once, that the God of the next is the God of the now. Sometimes we're inclined to believe the misnomer that there is a special group of people who receive suddenlies, and then another separate group who unfortunately have to wait. And keep waiting. And wait some more.

> Suddenlies represent divine interruptions that invade the process and change the outcome.

This belief is not true!

Waiting and suddenly are part of the same faith continuum. There is not a line separating patience from exuberance, expectancy from reception, and hope from thanksgiving. There is not a line for people who can wait and one for those who experience a suddenly.

Do your biblical due diligence and you will see from Genesis to Revelation the same people who experience a suddenly are the same people who were willing to wait on the Lord. If you have been waiting, then get ready. Because the next thing you are about to experience is a suddenly.

We know that there is an inheritance for those who wait. "Wait for the LORD and keep his way, and he will exalt you to inherit the land; you will look on when the wicked are cut off" (Psalm 37:34 ESV).

If you wait, you will be exalted to inherit the land that God has promised you. If you wait, you will inherit the promises—not the problems. If you wait, you will see your enemies cut off, defeated. Those who are willing to wait are those who qualify for a God-ordained suddenly.

Throughout Scripture, from beginning to end, suddenlies represent divine interruptions that invade the process and change the outcome. It may be unexpected or anticipated, but when God sends a suddenly, there is an abrupt outpouring of power that results in a radical change in recipients' plans.

Suddenly, a chariot of fire took Elijah up (see 2 Kings 2:11).

Suddenly, the psalmist said that all our enemies would be put to shame (see Psalm 6:10).

Suddenly, the tomb was empty because there was a great earthquake. "For an angel of the Lord came down from heaven and, going to the tomb, rolled back the stone and sat on it" (Matthew 28:2).

Suddenly, "a sound like the blowing of a violent wind came from heaven and filled the whole house where they were sitting" (Acts 2:2).

Suddenly, Peter was rescued and saved (see Acts 12:7).

All these suddenlies have one thing in common: all these people waited and persevered. They waited and worshiped. They waited and declared God's promises. They waited and obeyed. And then . . . *suddenly*!

What does this mean for you? If you've been proclaiming the promises of God, adhering to the Word of God, worshiping, praising, and praying, then you need to put a smile on your face because you should be expecting nothing less than a God-ordained suddenly.

There is a holy *suddenly* coming your way!

Suddenly, your family will be saved.

Suddenly, you and your loved ones will be delivered.

Suddenly, your body will be healed.

Suddenly, your promotion will take place.

Suddenly, the right person will enter your life.

Suddenly, your marriage will reach new heights.

Suddenly, your children will begin to thrive.

Suddenly, your breakthrough will burst forth.

Suddenly, the glory, the grace, the truth, the power, and the presence of Jesus will take over your life as you experience overflow and take over everything that's around you.

Why should you expect a suddenly? Because the same God who tells you to wait is the same God who will do it suddenly! Know without a doubt, the word of God will never fail (see Luke 1:37). Rest assured that God is faithful to keep all His promises (see Hebrews 10:23).

Wait for your *suddenly*. It's coming!

Inflammatory Speech

Not only did these believers experience a shift while in the Upper Room, not only did they feel the mighty wind descend upon them suddenly—they were on fire! "Then all at once a pillar of fire appeared before their eyes. It separated into tongues of fire that engulfed each one of them" (Acts 2:3 TPT).

Can you imagine? In case the wind didn't blow away any doubt about who had suddenly arrived and what was taking place, a pillar of fire spontaneously combusted in their midst! As if that were not stunning, staggering, and scintillating enough, that pillar of fire then separated into personalized pyrotechnics engulfing each individual in the room. This scene gives a whole new meaning to inflammatory speech.

Before we see what ignited from these tongues of fire, let's remember that this is not the first time a pillar of fire scorched the presence of God's people. When Moses, as instructed by God, led the Hebrew children out of Egypt, the Lord went before them by day in a pillar of cloud and by night as a pillar of fire (see Exodus 13:21). Approximately 1,500 years later, a heavenly pillar of fire once again shows up. But this time it is not to guide them toward the promise.

This time it is to fill them with the promise. Because there is a difference between you occupying the promise and the promise occupying you. When you are filled with God's Holy Spirit, not only do you live in the promise, but the promise lives in you. Which means the Promised Land for believers is not about *where* we are—it's about *who* we are.

Jesus called the Holy Spirit the promise (see John 14:15–17). The same Holy Spirit occupies you (see 1 Corinthians 3:16).

You experience this promise—which means you are a Promised Land! At Pentecost, the pillar of fire split up and descended upon them individually. From the pillar of fire to individual pillars. From the macro to the micro. Pentecost people must be people of fire, guided by the fire and sanctified by that fire. Infused with the fire in order to repeat the words of the prophet Jeremiah, "But if I say, 'I will not mention his word or speak anymore in his name,' his word is in my heart like a fire, a fire shut up in my bones. I am weary of holding it in; indeed, I cannot" (Jeremiah 20:9).

God's Word burns in us when we are filled with the same Spirit. We are compelled by the power in us to communicate the truth of the Gospel, the truth of who God is, the truth of His Spirit's power. We cannot be filled with the same Spirit that descended at Pentecost and remain silent.

So what happens when you cannot remain silent, when you have the fire of the Spirit in your bones? What happens when you have an individualized, personalized tongue of fire from the same Spirit engulf you? Your language changes!

Why would you suddenly need a new language? Why does being filled by the Spirit make you spiritually bilingual? Because we must know how to communicate the Word made flesh, Jesus Christ. We must allow the fire within us to burn through the lies and deception of the enemy.

We must speak the language of the Spirit because we know that if we want to change the culture, we must change the language. This truth emerges back in Genesis when we glimpse the power of a singular shared language.

> But the LORD came down to see the city and the tower the people were building. The LORD said, "If as one people speaking the same language they have begun to do this, then nothing they plan to do will be impossible for them. Come, let us go down and confuse their

language so they will not understand each other." So the LORD scattered them from there over all the earth, and they stopped building the city. That is why it was called Babel—because there the LORD confused the language of the whole world. From there the LORD scattered them over the face of the whole earth.

Genesis 11:5–9

Notice what God said was the reason for scattering them over all the earth. "If as one people speaking the same language they have begun to do this, then nothing they plan to do will be impossible for them." What's the problem with this kind of power? Human beings were not ready to handle the responsibility because they did not have the Holy Spirit yet. You need the guidance of the Spirit, the example of Jesus, and the instruction of the Father to use the unlimited power of spiritual speech.

When you are filled with the same Spirit, you speak what you have never spoken before. You receive the bilingual benefits of speaking fluently in the language of holiness, freedom, and power.

Change your language, change your world. We can change the culture if we change our language. Imagine speaking in the language of the Spirit. Imagine saying what the Holy Spirit wants to say. Imagine listening and comprehending the voice of God.

Why do you need a new spiritual language? Because you have to speak what you have never spoken in order to see what you have never seen.

> Change your language, change your world.

At Pentecost, it wasn't just any tongue—it was a tongue of fire from the Spirit of God. The tongues rested, sat upon them, and engulfed them. They could not stay silent with the language of heaven as it was burning in them on earth. This is the language of dominion, of spiritual authority, of healing power.

As Pentecost people, we can't speak just any language. We must speak the language of holiness, freedom, and power. We must speak a courageous language. Through the power of the same Spirit, God is giving you a new language.

It's time to speak truth and grace from the fire within you!

 THE SAME SPIRIT IN YOU

As you consider the transformative implications of Pentecost in your life, use the questions below to assist your reflection. Allow your responses to guide you into a time of prayer and stillness before God as you listen to the voice of the Spirit and converse with your heart. Keep in mind that you now have fluency in a spiritual language of empowerment, discernment, and insight. Like any language, you will find that practice enables you to become more attuned to the communication taking place.

So, take a deep breath, perhaps a few deep breaths, calm your mind, and quiet your heart. Then read through these questions and notice your responses. Make note of anything that jumps out at you or resonates in a particularly powerful way. Give some consideration to where you are right now in your life, the season as well as your journey of faith. Invite the wisdom and power of the same Spirit that raised Jesus from the dead—the same Spirit that descended on believers at Pentecost—to fill you yet again.

1. Where do you have Upper Rooms in your life, both past and present? How would you like the Holy Spirit to transform those painful places into thresholds of triumphant power?

2. What's something you're waiting on God to do in your life right now? What do you need to do in order to prepare for the *suddenly* He has for you?

3. How have you experienced the bilingual benefits of your new spiritual language through the filling of the Holy Spirit? What message has God placed on your heart lately?

PRAYER

Dear Lord, I am so grateful that You always fulfill Your promises. At Pentecost, You delivered the gift of the Holy Spirit that Jesus had promised, allowing us to experience Your eternal provision for all our needs. Thank You that I am filled with the same Spirit that descended in tongues of fire that day. Teach me Your vocabulary of grace so that my speech, in private and in public, may always reflect Your truth, Your goodness, Your mercy, and Your power. Give me patience as I expectantly wait for Your suddenly in my life! In Jesus' name, Amen.

PART 2

HEART

Inspired by the Spirit

And I will give you a new heart, and a new spirit I will put within you. And I will remove the heart of stone from your flesh and give you a heart of flesh. And I will put my Spirit within you, and cause you to walk in my statutes and be careful to obey my rules.

Ezekiel 36:26–27 ESV

5

A NEW SONG

Praising in the Same Spirit

When you worship in Spirit and truth, you praise God even when you are wounded.
　　Filled by the same Spirit of Pentecost power, your praise exalts heaven on earth!

I suspect my love of upbeat, contemporary praise and worship music results from my Puerto Rican roots. Traditional hymns are wonderful, of course, with many timeless melodies and memorable, biblically based lyrics. Sacred classical music is often sublime in its ability to evoke mood and imply narrative movement. Gospel music can stir the soul and voice the expressions of the human heart with unparalleled power and honesty.

But when I was growing up, I loved hearing music from many of the traditional Puerto Rican artists my parents would play on our record player. Yes, my family was into vinyl before being into vinyl was cool! Many of their records were instrumental albums reflecting the varied influences contributing to the music of our ancestral homeland.

These included salsa and merengue, plena and reggaeton, blending together instruments, rhythms, and upbeat tempos from the Caribbean, Africa, and Spain. Especially when extended family visited, this music inevitably transformed our living room into an impromptu dance floor, with my mother and father sometimes instructing the rest of us with their moves. Perhaps their example comes out even now when I preach, because sometimes I just can't stand still!

I also learned to appreciate the Latin jazz kings, particularly those of Puerto Rican descent like Tito Puenté and Ray Barreto. They impressed me with their artistry and originality, often leading their ensembles in *descarga*, an improvised jam session that was never the same way twice. I remember turning on the radio one day, probably in the late '70s or early '80s, and hearing the rock group Santana singing "Oye Cómo Va" and feeling so proud to recognize it from one of Tito Puenté's old albums that my parents used to play.

With such fond memories, I was not surprised when Latin music surpassed a huge milestone recently. In 2022, revenue from Latin music sales exceeded one billion dollars for the first time in the United States, according to the Recording Industry Association of America (RIAA).[1] Once considered a niche market, Latin music's popularity and sales have steadily increased each year over the past decade. Many new Latin artists push genre and style boundaries that attract a broad, diverse listening audience. According to a report by *Rolling Stone*, "Latin music continues to break further into the mainstream as one of music's preeminent genres, thanks to a growing number of global superstars."[2]

Perhaps Latin music contributed to my love of upbeat praise music because they both express a kind of joy, exuberance, and vitality. While they both reflect heart-stirring melodies, the music of praise is not limited to the worship band at church or your favorite contemporary Christian playlist. The music of praise flows inherently from a heart filled with the Holy Spirit.

Start Making Some Noise

Even before praise takes shape in music, even before words come together as lyrics, praise starts with a sound. Just as the arrival of the Holy Spirit at Pentecost began with a blast of what must have sounded like a tornado. "Suddenly they heard the sound of a violent blast of wind rushing into the house from out of the heavenly realm. The roar of the wind was so overpowering it was all anyone could bear!" (Acts 2:2 TPT).

They heard a sound—and what a sound! It was a sound that commanded their attention suddenly, a sound that could not be ignored, a sound that announced their anointing. Because being filled by the Holy Spirit always begins with a sound.

A sound is the initial evidence that a shift is taking place. A sound is the first indicator of transformation. A sound is the immediate response to revelation. From Genesis to Revelation and throughout the pages of the Bible, the greatest shifts began with a sound. With a sound, the Architect of the universe pushed back darkness when He said, "Let there be light" (Genesis 1:3).

With a sound, Joshua began the conquest of the Promised Land as the Israelites shouted and the walls came tumbling down (see Joshua 6:20). With a sound, Gideon's army defeated the Midianite

> Being filled by the Holy Spirit always begins with a sound.

marauders, breaking the jars that covered the fire torches as they shouted, "A sword for the LORD and for Gideon!" (Judges 7:20).

With a sound, the prophet Elijah prophesied the end of the drought by declaring, "I hear the sound of abundant rain coming our way!" And sure enough God's prophet then told Ahab, "Go, eat and drink, for there is the sound of a heavy rain" (1 Kings 18:41).

With a sound, the prophet Ezekiel saw a vision, the coming together of an army because the bones began to rattle and make some noise. "As I was prophesying, there was a noise, a rattling sound, and the bones came together, bone to bone" (Ezekiel 37:7).

With a sound, a blind man prompted Jesus to look his way and give him his sight by simply shouting, "Son of David, have mercy on me!" (Luke 18:38).

With a sound, Bartimaeus heard that it was Jesus of Nazareth and began to shout and say, "Jesus, Son of David, have mercy on me!" (Mark 10:47).

And guess who's coming back with a sound! "For the Lord himself will come down from heaven, with a loud command, with the voice of the archangel and with the trumpet call of God" (1 Thessalonians 4:16).

Spiritually speaking, a sound is the beginning of a shift. The greater the sound, the greater the shift. The louder the sound, the louder the shift echoes. A holy sound will push back darkness. A righteous sound will make the walls come down. A prophetic sound will release abundant rain. A courageous sound will confuse the enemy. A worshiper's sound will make Jesus look your way. A Spirit-filled believer's sound will become praise.

This is why we can't be silent. This is why we can't be complacent. This is why we can't be muted. The Church of Jesus Christ was born on Pentecost. The Church of Jesus Christ was born with a sound.

There is no such thing as a church without a sound. There is no such thing as Christianity on mute. There is no such thing as a silent Christ follower. There is no such thing as a complacent disciple of Jesus.

As people of the Spirit, if we don't hear the sound, then we must make a sound. And the sound that comes from the Spirit within us will always be louder than the sound that comes from the world around us. The Church must be louder than the culture. And by louder I don't mean irritating or abrasive. I don't mean harsh or annoying, even if the sound of our message may grate on ears unwilling to hear truth.

It's time for you to stop being so quiet and start making some noise. You can fill the world with the sound of grace, love, mercy, truth, and hope. You can fill the world with the joyful noise of the

Gospel. You can fill the world with the sound of redemption, renewal, and reconciliation. You were born with a sound, so you live with the sound. You were born again with a sound, so your life in the Spirit has a sound.

Outside your walls you can hear the sound of a broken world. Outside your home you can hear the sound of desperation. Outside your neighborhood you can hear the sound of a culture obsessed with cancellations, wokeness, offensiveness, unforgiveness, hypersensitivity, and victimization. You can hear the sounds of anxiety, depression, fear, consternation, angst, violence, hatred, chaos, pain, hurt, and brokenness.

But let not your heart be troubled. You are a Pentecost person. You are filled with the same Spirit. And the sound you make is praise!

Do You Hear What I Hear?

Sound is a mechanical wave, which means that it needs substance—such as air or water—to travel through and vibrate to produce sound waves. In space, there is no air, no atmosphere, so sound has nothing by which to travel. If someone were to scream in space, the sound wouldn't leave their mouths.

With this little audial lesson in mind, why don't more people hear the sound of the same Spirit in us that descended at Pentecost? Why doesn't culture listen to us? Why isn't the world becoming more like the Church? Why are they ignoring our sound?

Perhaps because they cannot hear us. What if the problem is not the sound, but the atmosphere? When we as Christians whine more than we worship, we don't create an atmosphere capable of carrying our sound—we create a vacuum. When we preach more about the problems than we do about the promises, that vacuum will not carry a holy sound.

But atmospheres shift when architects alter the environment.

I believe God is anointing men and women from every generation, not just to shift the current cultural atmosphere but to *create* a

God-honoring, spiritual atmosphere. If you are filled with the same Spirit that ignited tongues of fire on believers at Pentecost, then you are already altering your atmosphere. You may be shifting what's around you or creating a new atmosphere altogether—or both!

When your sounds come from the Spirit, you sing a new song into the spiritual silence of the world's culture. "Open up, O heavens, and pour out your righteousness. Let the earth open wide so salvation and righteousness can sprout up together. I, the LORD, created them" (Isaiah 45:8 NLT). To voice this new song, you don't need extra lung power, breath control, or a strong diaphragm; however, you must rely on the power of God's Spirit.

We are filled with a new sound because we know there's a difference between *feeling* God's presence and being *filled* with the Spirit of God. Not only does He want you to feel His presence—He wants you to be filled with His Spirit (see Ephesians 5:18). When we are filled, the sound we make resonates with the power of the cross and the Spirit of the empty tomb. Jesus paid the price so that we can go beyond a visitation of the Spirit to receive habitation by the Spirit.

Jesus came so that we can go from God with us to God in us. He shed His blood in order for His Spirit not just to move *over* us but for His Spirit to move *in* us. To paraphrase the observation of the brilliant British evangelist J. John, "It has been said that if Christmas is God *with* us and Easter is God *for* us then Pentecost God *in us*."[3]

The sound of Pentecost is God in you. And when the same Spirit is in you, you also hear what you haven't heard before. Do you hear what I hear? By faith in the name of Jesus and through the power of the Holy Spirit, I hear a sound!

I hear the sound of prophecy (see Ezekiel 37:7).

I hear the sound of greater things (see John 14:12).

I hear the sound of restoration (see Job 42:12–13).

I hear the sound of change (see Amos 9:13).

I hear the sound the enemy being crushed (see Romans 16:20).

I hear the sound of a wind like no other (see Acts 2:2).

I hear the sound of one Church bringing down the Goliath of hatred with the stone of love.

I hear the sound of one Church confronting the Herod of bigotry with the sword of the Spirit.

I hear the sound of one Church telling the pharaohs of the 21st century to let my people go so that they may worship.

I hear the sound of one Church that will remind all of humanity that our hands are made to create, our mouths are made to speak truth with love and to praise and worship, our hearts are made to forgive, and our knees are meant for prayer.

I hear the sound of one Church that will not be controlled by the donkey or the elephant but will only worship and bow before the Lamb who is the Lion of the tribe of Judah.

I hear the sound of one Church coming together that will not water down the Gospel, that will speak truth with love, preach the Word in and out of season, fulfill the Great Commission, make disciples, equip the saints, worship God in spirit and in truth, declare the year of the Lord's favor, and bring good news to the poor, freedom to the captives, and healing to the brokenhearted.

I hear the sound of one Church that will do justice, love mercy, and walk humbly before God.

I hear the sound of a Father-glorifying, Christ-exalting, Spirit-empowered, mountain-moving, devil-rebuking, demon-binding, atmosphere-shifting, world-changing, holy, healed, healthy, happy, humble, hungry, and honoring Church.

I hear the sound of people who are hungry for revival.

I hear the sound of abundant rain that brings an end to the spiritual, emotional, mental, and physical drought.

I hear the sound of a fresh outpouring of God's precious Holy Spirit.

I hear the sound of signs and wonders, healings and miracles.

I hear the sound of celebration as prodigal sons and daughters come back home.

I hear the sound of a new Great Awakening.

I hear the sound of freedom.

I hear the sound of free people who are free from sin, oppression, the past, systems, and structures that neglect the image of God in every single human being. I hear the sound of people who are free from injustice, free from false definitions, free from moral relativism, and free from fear.

My friend, do you hear what I hear?

Filling, Not Feeling

When you are filled by the same Spirit that arrived with the sound of a mighty wind, your own sound becomes a song of praise. Your praise defines and refines you. Your praise is not based on a feeling but on a filling. Because it's easy to feel like praising God and giving Him thanks and worshiping Him when you're enjoying the abundance of His blessings, when your family is healthy, when your car works, or when your bills are paid on time. When life seems to be working in your favor, your gratitude spills out in praise to the source of all goodness.

But it's tough to feel like praising God and worshiping Him when your life seems to be falling apart. When you're struggling hour to hour, day by day. When your body throbs with pain that no medication seems to alleviate. When your child's addiction weighs on your heart. When your car breaks down on the side of the road. When you don't have the money to pay last month's bills.

That's when you must remember: You don't praise because of a feeling but because of a filling! When you are filled by the same Spirit who raised Jesus from the dead, you know that all things work together for your good according to God's all-knowing plans. When you are filled by the same Spirit who descended on believers in the Upper Room, you know that you have supernatural power to endure natural disaster, personal crisis, family turmoil, and devastating loss.

Why? Because you choose to trust God even when you don't understand all that's going on around you. Because you believe His promises will be fulfilled. Because you know the same Spirit dwells in you.

We see this kind of praise throughout the Bible, particularly in Psalms and Lamentations, but two distinct scenes embody the paradox of praising while in pain. The first is one of my personal favorites because of how it inspires me to praise even when I'm perplexed. While on the road with the disciples teaching and preaching, Jesus received word that one of His best friends, Lazarus, was gravely ill (see John 11:3). His sisters, also dear friends of Jesus, had sent the message hoping that He would visit them and heal their brother.

You don't praise because of a feeling but because of a filling.

While He loved these three siblings (see John 11:5), Jesus did not change His schedule and go to Bethany where the trio lived for two more days. So, when Christ showed up, Lazarus had already been dead and entombed for four days (see John 11:17). By all appearances and human discernment, death had claimed Lazarus, and Jesus was too late. The dead man's sisters, Mary and Martha, grieving the loss of their brother, may also have felt disappointed, confused, perhaps even a little angry that Jesus had not arrived in time to prevent their beloved brother's death.

At this point, these two women had a choice in how they received the arrival of Jesus. They could refuse to see Him, remain in seclusion to grieve, and cut off contact with Him for failing to do what they had believed He was willing and able to do for them. Or they could choose to praise in the midst of their pain.

> When Martha got word that Jesus was coming, she went to meet him. But Mary stayed in the house. . . . Jesus told her, "I am the resurrection and the life. Anyone who believes in me will live, even after dying. Everyone who lives in me and believes in me will never ever die. Do you believe this, Martha?"

"Yes, Lord," she told him. "I have always believed you are the Messiah, the Son of God, the one who has come into the world from God." Then she returned to Mary. She called Mary aside from the mourners and told her, "The Teacher is here and wants to see you." So Mary immediately went to him. . . .

Jesus responded, "Didn't I tell you that you would see God's glory if you believe?"

John 11:20, 25–29, 40 NLT

Martha carried pain. The pain of grief. The pain of suffering. The pain of brokenness. The pain of loss. Yet the moment she heard Jesus was near, she ran. The moment she received notice of His presence, she left her sister's side, she left the other mourners, and she ran toward Him. Why? Because Martha knew that the presence of Jesus changes everything!

Martha had hard questions that only Jesus could answer. Her dear brother had died. The only One who could have healed him did not show up on time. Yet instead of going on social media to post her pain or texting her disappointment to all her contacts, Martha ran toward the Lord. Instead of engaging in the deconstruction of her faith, she ran toward the construction of her faith.

She was wounded, but she ran. She was in pain, but she ran. And when she encountered Jesus, she not only shared her pain but gave Him praise. She not only grieved but worshiped.

Can you hear her sobbing? "If only you had been here . . . because I know who You are! You are the Messiah. You are the Son of God. You are the Lord!"

In other words, even though I am hurting, I know who You are. Even though I am broken, I will not deny who You are because I know who You are. Even though I am shattered, I know who You are. And who You are is worthy of all my praise!

So much of the power of this interaction emerges from what is not said. Martha never said, "Well, I once thought You were the

Messiah. I used to believe You were the Son of God—until You let my brother die. Thanks for showing up too late!"

No, Martha did not express the bitter pain you or I may have felt. She did not speak in the past tense. She spoke in the present tense. I know who You are. You are the Messiah. You are the Son of God. This is the sound of praise emanating from a heart that's filled with faith even when broken. This is the sound of praise based not on circumstantial feelings but eternal, timeless, unchangeable truth.

What sound can we make to alter the atmosphere and change the world? We can sing a song of praise in the same Spirit that raised Jesus from the dead. We can sing a song of praise to the One who died for our sins, was buried, and rose again on the third day. The One who also raised Lazarus from the dead even after he had been buried.

Disciples of the risen Christ know who He is even in the midst of their pain. Spirit-filled believers do not focus on feelings to determine their praise. Those who are certain of Jesus' identity praise Him even in the midst of their suffering. This world will be changed by the sons and daughters of God. It will not be changed by those who think, hope, aspire, or wish but by those who know that Jesus is the Messiah, the Son of the living God. Regardless of what you're going through right now, I dare you to put down this book and shout, "Jesus, I know who You are!"

You are my Savior.

You are my deliverer.

You are my healer.

You are my rock.

You are my redeemer.

You are my going in, and You are my going out.

You are my purpose.

You are my passion.

You are my promise.

You are all that matters, and Your Spirit lives in me!

Sing a New Song

The second scene from Scripture that comes to mind when I consider the power of praising comes from Revelation. John describes his Spirit-inspired prophetic vision of being in heaven and being distressed because no one was worthy to open or read the scroll in God's right hand (see Revelation 5:1–3).

> Then I began to weep bitterly because no one was found worthy to open the scroll and read it. But one of the twenty-four elders said to me, "Stop weeping! Look, the Lion of the tribe of Judah, the heir to David's throne, has won the victory. He is worthy to open the scroll and its seven seals."
>
> Revelation 5:4–5 NLT

Then John watched as the slaughtered Lamb, the crucified Christ who triumphed over the grave, took the scroll from God and prepared to open it and read it. Even before that took place, however, those present fell down in worship before the Lamb. And like the Spirit-filled believers at Pentecost, they could not remain silent. They had to make sounds of praise with harps and sing a new song.

> You are worthy to take the scroll
>   and break its seals and open it.
> For you were slaughtered, and your
>   blood has ransomed people for God
> from every tribe and language and
>   people and nation.
> And you have caused them to become
>   a Kingdom of priests for our God.
> And they will reign on the earth.
>   Revelation 5:9–10 NLT

John may have blinked for a moment or shut his eyes in prayer because he tells us that when he looked again, the choir before him had dramatically expanded. From the song of the 24 elders and living creatures present, their song of praise was suddenly amplified by the voices of thousands and millions of angels around God's throne (see verses 11–12).

> Worthy is the Lamb who was slaughtered—
>   to receive power and riches
> and wisdom and strength
>   and honor and glory and blessing.
>   Revelation 5:12 NLT

And the sound of their angelic praise continued to be contagious. John reveals that he then heard every creature in heaven, on earth, under the earth, and in the sea all singing together. They sang, "Blessing and honor and glory and power belong to the one sitting on the throne and to the Lamb forever and ever" (verse 13 NLT).

John feared no one was worthy, capable, strong enough, or pure enough to open the sacred scroll. He wept bitter tears before they were transformed into tears of joy. He witnessed the singing of a new song.

In order to praise with a new song, we must allow God to transform our mourning into dancing, and we must recognize that the old song has played out. The record player is turning, but the needle has reached the last track in the vinyl. The old song no longer applies to where we are. The old song cannot express the power and freedom we have in the Spirit of God.

We've all heard the old song of broken promises and failed attempts, of hatred and racism, of intolerance and fear, and of division and strife. We've heard the antiquated song of cultural decadence and spiritual apathy with its mind-numbing melody and languishing lyrics, the irrelevant song of hopelessness and despair.

When you are filled by the same Spirit that inspired John with this heavenly vision, you cannot remain silent. You must sing a new song. And you are not alone singing this new song. This new song will not be sung exclusively by a black choir or a white ensemble, by a Latino band or an Asian soloist.

This new song will be sung by a multiethnic, divinely diverse choir washed snow white by the blood of the Lamb, Jesus Christ. This new song drowns out the fading chorus of captivity with its repulsive refrain. This new song raises the volume with prophetic power and a rhythm of revival. This new song reminds us where we have been, where we are, and where we are going. This new song praises God for always making a way.

For every Pharaoh, there is always a Moses.
For every Goliath, there is always a David.
For every Nebuchadnezzar, there is always a Daniel.
For every Jezebel, there is always an Elijah.
For every Herod, there is always Jesus.
For every devil that rises up against us, there is always a mightier God rising up for us.
This new song unites families in the love of Christ and the power of the Spirit.
This new song provides a prophetic prescription to end poverty.
This new song restores justice and brings freedom to the captives.
This new song never ends!

Soundtrack of Your Soul

The believers at Pentecost were all filled and equipped with the Holy Spirit (see Acts 2:4). They could not remain silent when the tongues of fire dispersed and engulfed each heart present in the Upper Room. They were filled with something—no, Someone!—they had never been filled with before.

They were not filled with emotion, they were filled with the Holy Spirit. They were not filled with a feeling, they were filled with the

Holy Spirit. They were not filled with a theory, they were filled with the Holy Spirit. They were not filled with an ideology, they were filled with the Holy Spirit.

Just so we are clear . . .

The Holy Spirit is not a denomination.

The Holy Spirit is not a network.

The Holy Spirit is not an emotion.

The Holy Spirit is not an experience.

The Holy Spirit is not a moment.

The Holy Spirit is not a service.

The Holy Spirit is not a conference.

The Holy Spirit is not an ideology.

The Holy Spirit is not a philosophy.

The Holy Spirit is not an app.

The Holy Spirit is the greatest influencer with the most followers on the planet!

There is no denying that other spirits want to rob our job and shatter our peace. Those spirits come after our children and attack the truth. The truth about God, the truth about gender, and the truth regarding science and math and logic and reason and basic human decency. There is a spirit attempting to distort authentic, holy, righteous love. But those spirits tremble at the name of Jesus.

No matter what you hear elsewhere—ABC, CBS, NBC, Netflix, Hulu, or Amazon Prime—the most powerful Spirit alive is not the spirit of moral relativism, cultural decadence, spiritual apathy, hedonism, bigotry, agnosticism, deconstructionism, perpetual victimization, hypersensitivity, or the cancel culture. The most powerful Spirit on the planet *was* and *still is*, back then and right now, the *Holy Spirit of almighty God*!

If you have that Spirit, shout like you have Him.

If you have that Spirit, praise like you have Him.

If you have that Spirit, worship like you have Him.

If you have that Spirit, fight like you have Him.
If you have that Spirit, pray like you have Him.
If you have that Spirit, rebuke the devil like you have Him.
And if you have that Spirit, then live like you have Him!

Here's what God's Word says is true:

"But you have received the Holy Spirit, and he lives within you" (1 John 2:27 NLT).

"Not by might, nor by power, but by my spirit, saith the LORD" (Zechariah 4:6 KJV).

"You will receive power when the Holy Spirit comes on you" (Acts 1:8).

"Where the Spirit of the Lord is, there is freedom" (2 Corinthians 3:17).

"The Spirit of God, who raised Jesus from the dead, lives in you" (Romans 8:11 NLT).

You have the same Spirit, my friend, and when you are filled with the same Spirit, praise is the soundtrack of your soul. In good times and hard times, in pain and in comfort, in joy and in sorrow, in grief and in gratitude, no matter what you're feeling, you praise from your filling.

Praise is your soul's soundtrack.

It's time to sing a new song!

THE SAME SPIRIT IN YOU

By now you know how the questions below are here to help you absorb and apply the powerful truths about the Spirit of God from this chapter. Take a few minutes and allow this time of reflection and prayer to serve as an opportunity for deeper intimacy with the Father, for closer connection with the Son, and for a fuller faith in the Spirit. No matter what you may be experiencing in your life right now, no matter what you may be feeling, allow your praise to come from your filling.

1. In general, what kind of music do you enjoy? What kind of music helps you praise and worship the Lord? Do the two have anything in common?

2. When have you experienced a painful loss or devastating disappointment and chose to praise as Martha did after Lazarus died? How does pain have an impact on your praise?

3. How would you describe the old song that continues to play in your mind and heart at times when you struggle? How would you describe the new song of praise God has placed in your heart through the Holy Spirit?

──────────── **PRAYER** ────────────

Dear God, thank You for placing a new song in my heart! Today, I no longer listen to the old songs of defeat, discouragement, and despair. Because I have the same Spirit within me that descended on believers at Pentecost, I can raise my voice to proclaim Your truth, Your grace, and Your love to everyone around me. Remind me when feelings start to overwhelm me that my filling by the Spirit remains strong. Worthy is Lamb! In Jesus' name, Amen.

6

A FEARLESS HEART

Waiting in—*Not on*—*the Same Spirit*

If you're waiting on a door to open, look for the blessing where you are.

Behind closed doors, Jesus shows up and prepares you for more!

Waiting can be scary.

As a father who waited while prayerfully pleading for his daughter's life as she battled COVID-19 in the hospital's Intensive Care Unit, I know how unsettling it can be. I'm not sure I've ever felt more helpless and powerless than while I was sitting and staring at my screen, watching Yvonne lie motionless in her hospital bed amidst so many cords and monitors. Because of the virus, the hospital had taken the necessary health and safety precautions, which did not permit visitors—not even direct family members—on the premises.

Clinging to my faith in our all-powerful God, I nonetheless struggled with so much uncertainty regarding the treatment and recovery of my precious daughter, a grown woman and mother herself. This was during the relatively early days of the pandemic when so many aspects remained tentative and unknown about the COVID-19 virus. Yvonne's respiratory system became so compromised that she was put on a ventilator and given super-steroids to help restore her lung capacity. Her doctors then recommended the treatment that precipitated her rapid recovery, an injection of antibodies derived from individuals whose immune systems had already beat the virus. Praise God that within hours of this treatment, Yvonne began a full recovery.

That's not, of course, my only experience with the fearful anxiety of waiting. As a pastor, I have visited many families and individuals as they endured seemingly interminable hours in a hospital lobby for their child to come through surgery. For their parent to be taken off life support. For an update from the surgeon about their spouse, brother, or sister who was rushed to the ER after the accident. For the medical results showing whether the chemo was working.

So much uncertainty.

So many doubts.

So few answers as quickly as we want them.

Fears that fray our nerves, trouble our minds, and jangle our hearts.

As you and I both know, waiting extends far beyond hospitals and doctors' offices.

Waiting can be scary.

Behind Closed Doors

I'll admit it. I have a hard time waiting. Perhaps you do too.

Waiting by faith is especially agonizing since we can't see how God is working or know what His answers to our prayers might be. Over the years, though, I've learned that *wait* and *suddenly* are part of the same faith continuum. Throughout Scripture, we see men and women of faith who waited: Abraham, Job, Esther, Daniel, Zechariah, Elizabeth, Mary, Samuel, Anna, the disciples, and so many others. Their wait was rewarded when it was least expected.

And *how* they waited prepared them for *what* they waited on.

They worshiped while they waited. They prayed, fasted, wept, and declared the promises of God. Their waiting literally changed the world, because people who wait in the Spirit are the people who experience a *suddenly* that arrives like a mighty, rushing wind.

Men and women filled with the Holy Spirit know that they wait *in* the Spirit—not *on* the Spirit. They know that waiting in the Spirit is not the same thing as waiting *for* God to do what we want Him to do, what we're hoping and praying He will do. Because the Spirit of God is always at work—in us, through us, around us, beyond us. This is true even when we have no evidence based on logic, probability, past experiences, or our human senses. Even when we're afraid of the unknown, of uncertain variables, or of imagined worst-case scenarios.

When we find ourselves waiting for God to open a door, however, we need to hit pause on our fear and confront it with our faith. Too often, we seem to be obsessed with both a church culture and an individual mindset driven by the idea of open doors. We talk about waiting for God to open a door, waiting on His power to make a way, and waiting on His guidance to reveal how we can go forward.

None of this is wrong.

But when we limit ourselves to open doors, we minimize the beauty and blessing of what takes place behind closed doors. We overlook what God is already doing where we are—to prepare us, educate us, equip us, and empower us. We miss out on the intimacy with God that takes places before the next door gets opened.

After the resurrection, Jesus appeared to His disciples not before an open door but behind a closed door.

> On the evening of that first day of the week, when the disciples were together, with the doors locked for fear of the Jewish leaders, Jesus came and stood among them and said, "Peace be with you!"
>
> John 20:19

The disciples were afraid—and for good reason. The Jewish authorities were spreading rumors that Jesus had not risen from the dead but that His body had merely been stolen by His followers to stage the appearance of a resurrection. Some of them had seen the risen Lord in person, but others, particularly Thomas, weren't so sure they believed what they heard.

And then suddenly, Jesus appeared and offered them—a key to open the door? A Xanax to calm their nerves? A pep talk on courage? No, Jesus appeared and offered them peace.

In our times of waiting, Jesus often meets us behind a closed door.

I'm convinced that sometimes closed doors have much more value than open doors. Closed doors usually proceed open doors. But in the meantime, we can experience the presence of Jesus and receive His peace. The supernatural, heavenly peace that surpasses human understanding. The peace that comes from waiting in the Spirit and not on the Spirit.

The disciples not only heard Jesus, not only saw Jesus, but at least one of them touched Him. He felt His wounds and saw the piercing in His side.

Spiritually speaking, before the disciples changed the world, they met with Jesus behind a closed door. In our times of waiting, Jesus often meets us behind a closed door. Sometimes God will even close a door in order to reveal something to you that otherwise you would not see.

A closed door with Jesus equals revelation.

A closed door with Jesus equals intimacy.

A closed door with Jesus equals an encounter like never before.

These disciples saw the wounds of the Messiah. They experienced His divine peace like a balm for their fear. My friend, amazing things happen behind closed doors. If you are filled with the Spirit but are waiting, and if you feel as if the door has closed in front of you, don't assume you're stuck in place. Don't curse the closed door. Don't disregard closed doors.

When you're waiting in the Spirit behind a closed door, it only means that you are about to touch Jesus and experience His grace in an unprecedented manner.

Believe by faith that your closed-door season prepares you for your open-door season. A closed-door season in which Jesus changes you often comes before the open-door season where you change the world.

Praise God for your open doors—and thank Him for your closed doors as well!

Anointing Determines Access

The disciples had gathered, their fear was palpable, and the door was closed. And Jesus appeared. He talked to them and spent time showing them His wounds. He made sure that each and every one of them received the reassurance they needed to know beyond a shadow of a doubt that He had risen from the grave. He chose to meet them behind closed doors and to give them peace. Before He sent the gift of the Holy Spirit at Pentecost, Christ wanted this intimate encounter to ground His disciples in the comfort of His living presence.

What if the closed doors you're behind right now serve His purpose?

What if the closed doors you're encountering are where you can experience His presence?

What if the closed doors you're facing are not there to block your path but to protect you?

What if God is protecting you from the elements that desire to rob, kill, steal, and destroy you?

What if the door is closed right now because God wants to show you something?

God is God of all doors—hospital doors, physical therapy doors, recovery room doors, bank doors, corner office doors, church doors, prison doors, bedroom doors, front doors, and back doors. "These are the words of him who is holy and true, who holds the key of David. What he opens no one can shut, and what he shuts no one can open" (Revelation 3:7).

Our God can open any door.

Our God can close any door.

And what He opens no one can close.

What He closes, no one can open.

Because if you look back at the closed doors in your life, you will see that they were not the obstacles you assumed them to be. It wasn't that the doors were not ready for you. It was that you were not ready to walk through those doors.

Your closed doors cannot stop Jesus from meeting you right where you are. The door was closed, the door was locked, and Jesus appeared. Could a locked door really stop the Son of God from entering? Could a closed door prevent the Savior of the world from showing up? Could a padlocked vault keep Jesus away from you?

Jesus overcame death. Through the power of the Holy Spirit, the same Spirit that lives in you, He returned to life. In other words, "Hey, friends, there was a stone in front of the tomb, and yet I came out. If I can go through a stone door, I can go through any door!"

Locked doors cannot stop someone with resurrection power.

Locked doors cannot hold back someone with resurrection power.

Listen, in the Church we hear people say, "I'm waiting for God to open the door." But wait! Did Jesus wait for the door to open? No!

Once you are crucified with Christ (see Galatians 2:20), once the old you dies (see 2 Corinthians 5:17), once you live in His resurrection power, you cannot be stopped by a closed door. "For since death came through a man, the resurrection of the dead comes also through a man. For as in Adam all die, so in Christ all will be made alive" (1 Corinthians 15:21–22).

Once you are born again, once you are filled with the same Spirit that raised Christ from the dead, once you die to live just like Jesus, your circumstances will not determine the outcome.

Instead, your anointing will determine your access. What you survived through the power of God will grant you access to restricted areas. Your grace-filled testimony will unlock your God-ordained destiny.

Because you overcame by the blood of the Lamb, because you overcame by the word of your testimony, because you experienced a breakthrough instead of being buried in what you went through, you are about to step in what was previously closed off. The old you could not get in, but the new you will walk right on through. Fear cannot prevent you from walking by faith in the power of the Holy Spirit.

Jesus appearing in a room where the doors stood shut likely prompted the query, "Where did You come from? How did You get in?" But after walking out of the empty tomb, He can go through any door.

People are about to begin asking you, "How did you get in? What are you doing here?"

They will want to know "If the manager said the company was no longer hiring, how did you get that job?"

"And if the doctor said what you had was terminal, how did you walk out with a clean bill of health?"

"If the bank was about to repossess your house, how did you end up paying off the mortgage?"

How?

And your only answer can be Jesus!

Your only answer is through the power of the Holy Spirit in your life.

Your only answer is by the same Spirit that raised Christ from the dead.

What Jesus did on the cross and what the Holy Spirit did in the tomb changed everything!

When He died, your old self died with Him.

When He rose up through the power of the Spirit, you rose up with Him.

When He walked through the doorway of the empty tomb, you came out with Him.

Others may not believe you're supposed to be here, but here you are.

And why are you able to be here because Jesus is here?

Because of a promise.

"For where two or three gather together as my followers, I am there among them" (Matthew 18:20 NLT). Closed doors cannot stop a loving God. The disciples gathered together, locked the door, and there was Jesus right among them.

Even when others close your door, Jesus still shows up.

Even when circumstances close your door, Jesus still shows up.

Even when you close the door yourself, whether intentionally or unintentionally, Jesus still shows up. No matter who you are, where you are, or what that door is made of, Jesus will always show up!

When Daniel was placed in the lions' den and they sealed it, God showed up.

When the Hebrew boys were in the fiery furnace, God showed up.

When the cold, lifeless body of Jesus was placed in a borrowed tomb, God showed up.

Just because a door closes does not mean it can stop God from showing up. Because a closed door cannot stop a resurrected Jesus.

No matter what door stands in your way, God is showing up for you.

Disclose the Divine

Behind closed doors when you're waiting in the Spirit, you are able to see the wounds that forgave your sins and the stripes that healed you. "Then he showed them the wounds of his hands and his side—they were overjoyed to see the Lord with their own eyes!" (John 20:20 TPT).

Jesus showed them His wounds and revealed His side where He was pierced. Why would He do that? We can be certain He was not showcasing His wounds as if to say, "Can you believe what they did to Me? Have pity on Me! I cannot believe I had to go through this! You know what? I'm going to start a hashtag movement—#NoMore Crosses!"

Quite the contrary. Jesus revealed His wounds and pierced side to confirm His identity. He was not showing what they did to Him; Jesus was showing what He did for *us*! He was not just showing His wounds and stripes. More importantly, He was showing the disciples their forgiveness—and your healing! Jesus revealed Himself to be the living testimony of triumph, the Word made flesh, Immanuel, God with us, the fulfillment of prophecy: "But he was pierced for our transgressions, he was crushed for our iniquities; the punishment that brought us peace was on him, and by his wounds we are healed" (Isaiah 53:5).

When you look at the wounds of Jesus, you see your forgiveness. When you look at the stripes of Jesus, you see your healing.

When you experience the presence of Jesus, you are dead to sin and alive for righteousness. "He personally carried our sins in his body on the cross so that we can be dead to sin and live for what is right. By his wounds you are healed" (1 Peter 2:24 NLT). By showing up behind closed doors with His disciples, He makes an implicit declaration of eternal truth. "They tried everything, and yet here I am. I was beaten and bloody, and yet here I am. I was parched and pierced, and yet here I am. I was mocked and denigrated, and yet here I am. And if I did it, *you* can do it."

My friend, when you find yourself in a place where the door is closed, where you feel stuck, where you assume you are waiting on God, waiting on the Spirit to move, I challenge you to stop and consider what the Lord has done for you. Don't let your wounding stand in your way. Don't allow your wounding to leaving you waiting when you already have the same Spirit within you that raised Christ from the dead.

And realize that you, too, have something to show and something to share with those around you. You may wonder, "Should I really disclose what happened to me? Do I have to reveal how my wounding happened?" And here's your answer: Jesus paid the price so that you can show something else.

You don't need to talk about Pharaoh's soldiers chasing you out of Egypt. You only need to reveal the parting of the Red Sea. You only need to disclose the divine mercy, grace, and healing you have received in Christ through the power of the Holy Spirit because of the love of the Father. When the holy fire of God's Spirit ignites and fuels your faith, you illuminate His redemption. Disclose the divine!

Christ showed His wounds so that you can show your healing.

Christ showed His piercing so that you can show your peace.

Christ showed His power so that you can show you have the same Spirit in you.

Instead of saying, "Look what my ex did to me," open your mouth and declare, "Look what my Lord did for me!"

Instead of saying, "Look at what the abuse did to me," open your mouth and declare, "Look what my Lord did for me!"

Instead of saying, "Look at all I've been through," open your mouth and declare, "Look where my Lord has brought me!"

When you're waiting in the Spirit, you stop focusing on the pain to focus on the promise. Complaining about what was done to you only highlights how the enemy tried to stop you. Stop subsidizing the devil's marketing budget. Your brand message cannot be more powerful than, "Look what the Lord has done. I am forgiven and I am healed."

Peace, Not Panic

Christ not only showed the disciples His wounds but greeted them with a double dose of *shalom*. "Jesus repeated his greeting, 'Peace to you!' And he told them, 'Just as the Father has sent me, I'm now sending you'" (John 20:21 TPT). Why repeat His greeting to them? For what reason do you repeat a greeting when you are with people you love? Imagine seeing your children or grandchildren who live in another state or a beloved friend who has been away. "It's so good to see you!" you exclaim. "It's *sooo* good to see you!"

Repetition adds emphasis. It conveys what you use italics and all capitals for when you're emailing and texting. Jesus wanted to make sure that His disciples knew it was really Him, and He wanted to make sure they knew He brought them peace.

As you may know, the Hebrew word for peace is *shalom*. But this idea of peace carries a much more comprehensive, pervasive sense of well-being than we might expect. When we think of peace, we usually think of calm and quiet, or the absence of turmoil, conflict, and battle. But the Jewish notion of shalom-peace is about experiencing wholeness, being complete, having balance, and knowing fulfillment. Shalom-peace is redemptive restoration and stability that cannot be shaken.[1]

This was not the first time Jesus told His followers that He brought them peace. In fact, He had made a pointed distinction. "I leave the gift of peace with you—my peace. Not the kind of fragile peace given by the world, but my perfect peace. Don't yield to fear or be troubled in your hearts—instead, be courageous!" (John 14:27 TPT). Notice the difference? Worldly peace is fragile and can disappear with a harsh word, an angry glance, or a physical blow. Heavenly peace is perfect and inspires the kind of courage that dispels fear.

Jesus mentioned the relationship between His peace and our courage another time as well.

> And everything I've taught you is so that the peace which is in me will be in you and will give you great confidence as you rest in me. For in this unbelieving world you will experience trouble and sorrows, but you must be courageous, for I have conquered the world!
>
> John 16:33 TPT

Christ's teachings facilitate divine peace and provide great confidence—supernatural, spiritual, surpassing confidence—as we rest in Him.

This kind of confidence reminds me of a cultural custom I've observed in South American communities. As soon as children can walk and talk, they are taught what they should do if they become separated from their parents or family while out in public. Once a child realizes he or she has become separated, the child goes to the nearest adult and explains that he is lost and needs help finding his father or mother. The adult, well aware of the community custom, picks up the child and asks his or her name. Then the adult begins shouting, "Lost!" followed by the child's name.

Everyone around them immediately picks up the chant and begins clapping loudly. They continue the attention-getting display until the relieved parents come forward to reunite with their child. There are numerous examples of this clever and compassionate cultural phenomenon online. One recent clip I observed showed a young boy in a crowded plaza in Buenos Aires, Argentina. Little Juan Cruz somehow got separated from his father, Eduardo, only to be reconnected a few minutes later thanks to the well-known system in place.[2]

What's striking to me is the way no one panics—not the child, the chosen adult, others around, or the child's caregiver. Even while waiting to be reunited, because of their trust in the kindness of the community, they have confidence. What a beautiful reminder of the confidence we have through the peace of Christ.

We are not lost, however, but found! When we are waiting in the Spirit, we don't need to panic or worry or give into the fear. We have the peace of our Lord inside us. We have confidence in knowing that His Spirit dwells within us. The same Spirit of resurrection power now empowers us. We have full access to the peace of Christ regardless of what side of a door we're on.

No matter what you're waiting on, you can experience the peace that will never make sense to the world because with God all things are possible. Closed doors can't separate you from Jesus. The same Spirit is in you. His peace leaves no room for panic. Regardless of your trial, tribulation, or turmoil, your peace remains intact.

Peace in the midst of pain.

Peace in the midst of peril.

Peace in the midst of persecution.

Peace in the midst of pandemics.

Peace in the midst of personal injury.

Peace in the midst of professional dismissal.

As you wait and wonder behind closed doors, Jesus greets you with a double portion of shalom. You have peace right now even if you don't know when the door will open or how you will walk through it. You have peace right now even if you don't know what's waiting for you on the other side of that closed door.

Peace is resting in His victory.

You don't need to panic—you have peace. Jesus has taken away the power this world has to defeat us. He has conquered it for us. Peace is resting in His victory. In Jesus' name, you have peace. In God's Spirit, peace is inside you.

Peace in your marriage.

Peace in your children.

Peace in your job.

Peace in your relationships.

Peace in your body.

Peace in your mind.

Peace in your heart.

Welcome Your Wait

After visiting His disciples behind closed doors but before He ascended into heaven, Jesus told them not to leave too soon. He had a gift for them already prepared for delivery via Pentecost Prime to an Upper Room in Jerusalem.

Don't leave Jerusalem, but wait here until you receive the gift I told you about, the gift the Father has promised. For John baptized you in water, but in a few days from now you will be baptized in the Holy Spirit!

Acts 1:4–5 TPT

Have you ever visited someone or attended a party and had them stop you on your way to exit? "You can't leave until you get the gift I have for you," they might say. "Don't go anywhere! I'll be right back with it. And this gift is worth the wait!" Multiplied on a scale that exceeds comparison, this message gave Christ's followers cause for pause.

They wanted to leave.

It would have been logical to leave.

It made sense after the crucifixion of their Master to get out of Jerusalem before the authorities came looking for them. They probably wondered, "Are we next to be falsely arrested and killed?"

It made sense after the empty tomb for them to leave. "They're saying that we stole the body! They will want to question us at the very least."

Well aware of their fear, Jesus said, "Don't leave yet! My present for you is more than worth the wait."

Why did He want them to stay? Couldn't Jesus have sent the Holy Spirit to them no matter where they were?

Because places matter. Because not every place is blessed. Not every atmosphere facilitates the glory. Where you are has an impact on how you are. Your location will either obstruct or facilitate revelation.

Jerusalem was not just any city. Jerusalem was the city that David conquered.

The king and his men marched to Jerusalem to attack the Jebusites, who lived there. The Jebusites said to David, "You will not get in here; even the blind and the lame can ward you off." They thought, "David cannot get in here."

2 Samuel 5:6–7

David didn't have to consider their threats because God's peace gave him confidence. "Oh, yeah? Watch this!" he may have thought. The last laugh was clearly had by David, who had God's Spirit upon him.

But wait, there's more! Why Jerusalem? There are two miracles that Jesus performed within the city walls of Jerusalem. We're told in John chapter 5 how He healed the lame man, and we are told in John chapter 9 how He gave sight to the blind man at the Pool of Siloam. The Jebusites said even the blind and the lame could keep him out. Jesus dealt with the two things that their enemy said would impede God's children from stepping in and claiming the city of Jerusalem.

Jesus took care of both of those, and so much more.

Through the power of the same Spirit in you, you are just as unstoppable. I'm here to tell you that Jesus has already dealt with everything that had the ability to stop you, hinder you, obstruct you, impede you, or block you from experiencing the fulfillment of His promise. Jesus took care of everything that could hold back the door that now needs to be opened. Jesus took care of everything that tries to prevent you from resting in His confidence and peace.

Your fearful heart—remember, the disciples gathered in that room behind locked doors because they were afraid—has been transformed into a fearless heart. Nothing can impede you from living a holy, healed, healthy, happy, humble, hungry, honoring life. Jesus took care of everything that would have blocked you and your children and your children's children from living an abundant, eternal, and new life.

So don't leave now! Do not quit waiting and try to leave your Jerusalem. Jesus is right there with you. His Spirit is within you. Don't decide to go before you see what God wants to do for you, what He wants to give you, how He wants to bless you.

If you're tired of waiting, take heart.

If you're afraid of what happens next, fear not.

If you're disappointed by a closed door, just wait.

Do not leave Jerusalem because the gift is worth the wait.

If you leave town now, you don't get it.

If you can't wait, you won't get it.

Yes, waiting is hard. Waiting in line, waiting on good news, waiting on bad news, on medical test results, on decisions to be made, jobs to be offered, houses to sell, loans to come through, cars to be fixed, and children to return home. Waiting requires supernatural power in order to persevere. It is a good thing that you have the power of the same Spirit inside of you.

Welcome your wait because the Holy Spirit will sustain, nourish, and empower you. You will be able to wait in the Spirit until God's appointed time. "But those who hope in the Lord will renew their strength. They will soar on wings like eagles; they will run and not grow weary, they will walk and not be faint" (Isaiah 40:31).

Welcome your wait because the gift Jesus told His followers to anticipate has already arrived at your address. God's Word confirms:

> "In the last days," God says, "I will pour out my Spirit upon all people. Your sons and daughters will prophesy. Your young men will see visions, and your old men will dream dreams."
>
> Acts 2:17 NLT

God has poured out His Spirit upon you.

Even while you wait behind a closed door, you have the greatest gift. It is a gift that first arrived in an Upper Room to 120 people who gathered in the name of Jesus. Now that same Spirit dwells in you. Without a doubt, the gift is yours.

You got the gift—*so open it!*

THE SAME SPIRIT IN YOU

As you've grown accustomed to by now, the questions below can help you process and apply the powerful principles of waiting *in* the Spirit, and not *on* the Spirit, in this chapter. Consider the closed doors you may be facing right now and ask God to meet you where you are with His peace, His confidence, and His perfect plan and timing. Then spend a few minutes opening your heart before Him, listening to the voice of the same Spirit as you pray and worship.

1. What are some closed doors you're facing in your life right now? How would you describe your current season of waiting?

2. When has Jesus appeared behind closed doors with you lately and filled you with His perfect peace? How is His peace different from peaceful moments or feelings you've experienced?

3. What dispels your fear when you're struggling with uncertainty and an unknown future? How does waiting in the power of the Holy Spirit affect your fears? Why?

──────────────── **PRAYER** ────────────────

Dear Jesus, I am so glad that You are more powerful than any fear I face. Today, please remind me, Lord, that I have Your perfect peace in me and Your presence with me no matter what might happen. Give me the courage that comes from the confidence I have in You. Grant me patience to trust You and wait on the Father's timing for opening or closing the doors before me. I offer You praise for giving me the greatest gift, the same Spirit that raised You from the dead, and I worship You even in the midst of waiting. In Jesus' name, Amen.

7

A VICTORIOUS HOPE

Overcoming in the Same Spirit

God's glory shines when you walk by faith and overcome in
His Spirit!
If you want to experience God's power in your life, then
you must elevate Jesus above everything and everyone else.

G rowing up in Pennsylvania, I remember passing by the rescue
mission where the words *Jesus Saves!* were proclaimed in
neon letters bright enough to light up the entire block. At
the time the illumination of this truth remained more of a literal
luminary than a timeless tenet of biblical certainty. I suspect for
many of us living in that area those two bright words became part
of the landscape, something overlooked by familiarity.

Years later, I was driving into New York City, and after crossing
the Holland Tunnel, there were those same two words: *Jesus Saves!*
This time they jumped out at me not with the neon glare of my
hometown rescue mission but with the elaborate, artistic grace of
graffiti. Juxtaposed against the bustling traffic going into the city,
those two words demanded attention—for those who had eyes to see.

You've probably glimpsed those words on various signs and store-fronts as well. They might be on a church message board or a minis-try welcome sign. They might have been spray-painted on a vacant building or scrawled in marker on a subway wall. You might have noticed them, or they may have become part of the scenery.

As a believer, you know they are true. You understand that those two words express that our victory in Christ comes through our salvation. But what exactly does it mean to be saved? How does our salvation establish our victory?

Let's unpack this flammable phrase and how it ignites the holy fire of God's Spirit in our lives.

Salvation Dawning

Even before God sent His Son to die on the cross for our salvation, saving His people has always been who He is and what He's all about. God has always been a savior and a saving God. He saved Joseph from dying because of his brothers' betrayal. God saved the Hebrews from permanent Egyptian captivity. The Lord saved Elijah from Jezebel, Daniel from the lions, and the Hebrew boys from a fiery furnace. God saves.

Yet all of us require salvation way beyond circumstances, enemies, and external threats. This is why God sent His beloved Son to live, die, and defeat death once and for all, saving us from our sins and securing for us the power of His Spirit within us. This is the choice we make when we accept the free gift of grace—that provides de-liverance from sin and its consequences—and walk by faith. This is the Gospel definition of *salvation*, which Paul succinctly expresses so well. "For the wages of sin is death, but the gift of God is eternal life in Christ Jesus our Lord" (Romans 6:23).

We have received what Isaiah foretold about God's people. "Then your light will break forth like the dawn" (Isaiah 58:8). This is not simply a poetic simile or an Instagram image of a pink and yellow sunrise. Once God created the heavens and earth, He set the planets in motion around the sun in our solar system resulting in night and day based on earth's rotational orbit. For us on earth, we see the sun rise every morning and the sun set every night. Since creation, this natural trajectory perpetuates the continuity of linear time for humanity.

My point, then? That the rising of the sun is inevitable as long as the Lord permits it. For every human being who has lived thus far in the history of our world, the rising of the sun has remained

> Without salvation, nothing else matters.

a constant, a predictable certainty. So when Isaiah says that "your salvation will come like the dawn," he means that it's certain, reliable, and already established.

Salvation is fundamental to our faith.

Salvation is foundational to our identity in Christ.

Salvation is the fulfillment of God's promise to send His Spirit.

Everyone needs to be saved. Everyone requires salvation. Because without salvation, you will not have eternal life.

I don't care how good you are, what social justice cause you fight for, how much money you give to the poor, who you know, or which church you attend. It doesn't matter how many seminary degrees, PhDs, and MDs you have framed on your walls. It's irrelevant whether you volunteer at the homeless shelter, stock the food pantry, teach the Sunday school class, or lead the small group.

Without salvation, nothing else matters. Without salvation—keep in mind that this is not my opinion but God's Word—we are born sinners, the result of the original disobedience of Adam and Eve in the Garden of Eden. Because we are all born sinners, the inevitable result is eternal death, perpetual hell, and permanent separation from almighty God.

Again, I am just the messenger for this message, but permit me to reiterate:

Without salvation, eternal death.

Without salvation, eternal condemnation.

Without salvation, eternal hell.

Without salvation, eternal separation from God.

But—and thank You, Lord, for that three-letter contrarian conjunction "but"—glory be to God that "the gift of God is eternal life in Christ Jesus our Lord" (Romans 6:23).

Salvation is God's free gift.

Salvation has no price but remains priceless.

Salvation costs *nothing* and means *everything*.

Victory in Present Tense

Jesus Saves expresses the victory of salvation we have in Christ. This little phrase also conveys the way we find ourselves in trouble, in danger, in calamity, or in despair only to encounter the redeeming power of God's Spirit, only to realize He has gone before us and is already at work in our lives. God's Spirit is involved in the details of our lives in countless ways.

When the Holy Spirit dwells in us—the same Spirit that raised Jesus from the dead—we experience not only resurrection power but redemption power. We discover that we are no longer bound by the darkness because we are now illuminated from within by heavenly light. We discover that no longer are we enslaved to destructive habits because we have been set free from the power of sin over us. We discover that no longer are we limited to what we can do in our own power because now we have Christ's power to overcome death inside us.

Long before Pentecost, God's people were told to expect these discoveries. "Then your light will break forth like the dawn, and your healing will quickly appear; then your righteousness will go before you, and the glory of the LORD will be your rear guard" (Isaiah

58:8). The Lord's chosen prophet Isaiah spoke these words of God's truth to His people while they were in captivity. The Israelites were defeated spiritually, emotionally, psychologically, financially, and physically. At this time, God's people were begging and pleading for even the smallest spark of hope, likely wondering if they would ever experience victory of any kind again.

But then came the word of the Lord.

Still today, there is nothing more powerful than, "Thus saith the Lord!"

And I'm convinced this prophetic word from Isaiah still applies to us today even as we live in its fulfillment as overcomers in the power of the Holy Spirit. This word of the Lord brings heaven to earth and enables you to overcome your hell. This word brings wisdom and truth to dispel and defeat the diabolically fabricated lies of the enemy in your life.

Why do I believe this? Because God said it! "If you belong to Christ, then you are Abraham's seed, and heirs according to the promise" (Galatians 3:29). Let's see then. Are you Christ's? Check. Okay, then are you Abraham's seed? Check. And therefore, heirs to the promise? Check. Yes, yes, and yes!

If you're struggling with the challenges of life, the temptations of the enemy, and the residual baggage of your past, then you need to realize the victorious hope of your salvation in Jesus Christ. Owning the hope of your salvation means that you already know what comes next. No matter what you might be experiencing right now, you have the same Spirit within you that won the victory over death through the resurrection of Jesus. Your victory is in present tense.

So what's next for you? What's next for your family, what's next for your children, and what's next for your loved ones? Let me tell you with biblical certainty what's next. If you want to know what to expect, then it's time to let the word of the Lord, the promise of the Prince of Peace, take root in your heart.

This is God's word for you and your family.

This is God's word for you and the people you love.

This is God's word for you and your children and your children's children.

In Christ, with Christ, for Christ, you have victory.

Victory is not coming.

Victory is not on the way.

Victory is not a futuristic concept to be embraced upon its arrival.

Victory is not the conditional result of some future battle.

The victory has already been secured.

The victory has already been given.

The victory has already been implemented.

"But thanks be to God! He gives us the victory through our Lord Jesus Christ" (1 Corinthians 15:57).

We received victory when Jesus died on the cross.

We received victory when Jesus resurrected from the dead.

We received victory when He filled us with the Holy Spirit; therefore, my friend, stop praying for victory. Quit fasting in the hope victory will come. No longer do you need to praise and worship so that you can know victory. You will not be victorious one day—you are victorious today! The moment you are born again you are automatically permanently and perfectly victorious. Victory is already yours.

Don't pray for victory—pray *from* victory.

Don't praise for victory—praise *from* victory.

Don't fast for victory—fast *from* victory.

Victory is already yours.

You are victorious. Wherever you look, you will see victory. "For the LORD your God is the one who goes with you to fight for you against your enemies to give you victory" (Deuteronomy 20:4). Wherever you go, you will experience victory. "For everyone born of God overcomes the world. This is the victory that has overcome the world, even our faith" (1 John 5:4).

Whether you look right or left, go east or west, jump up and down, you will find victory. Victory means you have no other choice but to overcome. To overcome is to defeat, to conquer, to triumph, to win. When you are filled with the Holy Spirit, you have no other choice but to overcome.

Abraham overcame his lies.

Joseph overcame the pit and the betrayal of his brothers.

Moses overcame Pharaoh, his temper, and his past.

Joshua overcame Jericho, the disobedience of his troops, and his fear of being alone when his mentor died.

Gideon overcame the threshing floor.

Samson overcame his pride, his lack of respect for the anointing, and Delilah's deception.

David overcame Saul's spear, a bear, a lion, a giant, and his own moral turpitude.

Esther overcame the haters.

Daniel overcame the lions.

The Hebrew boys overcame the furnace.

Job overcame the loss of everything.

Peter overcame the cursing of his blessing.

Paul overcame the shipwreck and the snake bite.

And Jesus—Jesus overcame darkness, death, and defeat.

Jesus overcame everything!

His victory is your victory.

You are not a victim.

You are not the devil's punching bag.

You are not cursed, condemned, or criticized.

You are—in Christ, by Christ, for Christ—an *overcomer*!

Eyes of Your Heart

Even when you know you are an overcomer, even when you have already overcome so much, you may still struggle. Experiencing the hope of victory you already have can be difficult to embrace at times. You know you already have the victory, but you struggle to own it by faith when it is not yet manifest visibly. That's when you must see with the eyes of your heart and not merely the eyes in your head.

Paul told believers at Ephesus, "I pray that the eyes of your heart may be enlightened in order that you may know the hope to which he has called you, the riches of his glorious inheritance in his holy people" (Ephesians 1:18).

Why does Paul pray that their eyes may be enlightened? So that they will know the hope to which God has called them. So that they will experience the riches of God's glorious inheritance—where?—in His holy people. This is spiritual enlightenment, my friend. This is allowing the Spirit within you to look beyond what the eyes in your body can envision.

When you look with the eyes of your heart, you can see the invisible reality of victory because of the power of the Spirit within you. What you look upon may resemble defeat temporarily. What attracts your attention may appear to be dormant, stagnant, or inactive. What disrupts your life when it blindsides you may seem to knock you down. But no matter what you experience, when you look with the eyes of your heart, you will still see victory.

When you look at your children and your children's children, you will see victory.

When you look at your marriage, you will see victory.

When you look at your health report, you will see victory.

When you look at your financial accounts, you will see victory.

When you look at your resumé, you will see victory.

When you look at your *now*, you will see victory.

When you look at your *next*, you will see victory.

From this moment on, you will pray from victory.

From this moment on, you will praise from victory.

From this moment on, you will worship from victory.

The prophetic word in Isaiah 58:8 cannot and will not be denied. It was true then, and it remains true now.

You are stepping into not just a season, but into a *lifetime* of victory.

Victory defines you and your family and your loved ones as you pursue righteousness in the name of Jesus. Victory describes who you are as a new creature in Christ, God's still-in-progress masterpiece, and more than a conqueror. Victory determines how you measure your steps each day as you follow the guiding voice of the Spirit within you.

You will live in and with the victory of salvation all the days of your life!

This Joy You Have

Then why, you might ask, does your life seem more overwhelming than overcoming? Why don't you experience the joy of the Lord the way your heart longs to know?

Sometimes we get so caught up in our lives, in our families and our careers, in our personal struggles and private battles, that we overlook the unshakable foundation of our faith. Even churches lose sight of this most important aspect: making sure that every member of the flock has a personal, intimate relationship with the Good Shepherd, Jesus Christ. We often get so bogged down in the minutia of life and peripheral issues of human existence that we neglect the most important message that can come out of any believer's mouth, any church's pulpit, any event's podium.

Too often, we're focused on what is nonessential instead of what is essential. We get caught up in twelve steps to feeling good, ten steps to looking better, seven steps for financial prosperity, five steps for better relationships, and three steps for eating all you want without counting calories. We get excited about mastery before we know the Master.

No, the most important message we can and will ever preach is simple:

> For God so loved the world that he gave his only begotten Son that whosoever believes in him will not perish, shall not perish, cannot perish, but will have everlasting, eternal life! God sent his Son into the world not to judge the world, but to save the world through him.
>
> John 3:16–17, author's paraphrase

Hallelujah!

Jesus did not come to condemn.

Jesus did not come to establish a religious order.

Jesus did not come to initiate a social movement.

Jesus did not come to occupy political office.

Jesus came to save you.

Jesus came to save your children.

Jesus came to save your children and your children's children.

Jesus came to save your family.

Jesus came to save your community.

Jesus came to save your generation.

He did not come to condemn you.

Jesus did not come to send you to hell.

Jesus came to save you from hell.

To save you from eternal condemnation.

To save you from your past.

To save you from yourself.

In other words, our God saves.

No other god saves. You read that correctly—no other god saves!

With great deference and all due respect to other teachings and other religious ideologies, consider this:

Have you ever heard that Buddha saves you?

Have you ever heard that Mohammed saves you?

Have you ever heard that Confucius saves you?

Have you ever heard that communism saves you?

Have you ever heard that capitalism saves you?

Have you ever heard that consumerism saves you?

Have you ever heard that atheism saves you?

The only one who can save you is Jesus.

Thanks be to God that you have the victory of salvation that only comes from Christ. "Salvation is found in no one else, for there is no other name under heaven given to mankind by which we must be saved" (Acts 4:12).

There is no greater joy than the joy of salvation.

There is no greater peace than the peace of salvation.
There is no greater promise than the promise of salvation.

I think of the gospel hymn "This Joy I Have," written by the iconic Shirley Caesar. It declares that the joy we have as believers doesn't come from the world, which means the world cannot take it away. The Spirit in us—the same Spirit that hovered and covered the world before it was formed, the same Spirit that raised Jesus from the dead, the same Spirit that descended on 120 believers at Pentecost—that Spirit is in us. The world didn't give us that Spirit and the world can never take that Spirit away from us. Jesus won the victory and set you free.

When you are saved you walk a little differently.
When you are saved you talk differently.
When you are saved you give differently.
When you are saved you love differently.
When you are saved you praise differently.
When you are saved you pray differently.
When you are saved you live differently.

My friend, you have a glorious hope because of the victory of your salvation. Not wishful thinking. Not castles in the air. Not daydreams that fade away. A living, glorious, victorious hope.

Because of our salvation, Paul said not only do we "boast in the hope of the glory of God . . . but we also glory in our sufferings, because we know that suffering produces perseverance; perseverance, character; and character, hope" (Romans 5:2–4). Notice the way Paul acknowledges that we're going to suffer and highlights the unexpected—suffering helps us overcome through the power of God's Spirit. How do I know this? Paul anticipated this question: "And hope does not put us to shame, because God's love has been poured out into our hearts through the Holy Spirit, who has been given to us" (verse 5).

Your hope is real.

Your hope is victorious.

Is That Who I Think It Is?

When you are saved, you want to elevate Jesus above everything and everyone else. You want the world to know who He is and how much He loves them—enough to die for them. You want them to see His Spirit within you and the transformative impact He has on your life. You want everyone around you to recognize that Jesus is unlike anyone they have ever met or will ever meet.

In one of my favorite scenes from the life of Jesus, we glimpse a literal, not just figurative, display of the singular, sacrificial, supernatural person and power of Christ. It happened during a private retreat when Jesus had taken Peter, James, and John up to a mountain in order to pray together. But what happened once they were there was probably not the experience those three disciples expected.

> And as he was praying, the appearance of his face was transformed, and his clothes became dazzling white. Suddenly, two men, Moses and Elijah, appeared and began talking with Jesus. They were glorious to see. And they were speaking about his exodus from this world, which was about to be fulfilled in Jerusalem.
>
> Luke 9:29–31 NLT

This scene revealed a pre-resurrection manifestation of Jesus' glory not only in Spirit but in His body. While Jesus was praying, His face was transformed—glowing, radiating, and beaming. His clothes brightened as well, not just white but *dazzling* white. Suddenly—and there's that word again—suddenly, two of the greatest prophets in Jewish history, Moses and Elijah, appeared and began talking to Jesus. We're even told what they were discussing: how Christ would soon leave this world following the fulfillment of prophecy about His death and resurrection.

This is not merely a surreal scene—it was *glorious* to see.

Why? Because it reflects God's glory in visible, dramatic, neon-bright fashion. This is heaven touching earth. This is Jesus on the red carpet. This is the Messiah with the spotlight of heaven shining on Him.

Then, suddenly, He's not alone—we've got guest stars with cameos. In case you're not fully immersed with Hollywood lingo, a cameo is a small character part in a play or movie performed by a distinguished actor or celebrity in a role often created just for them to make a dramatic impact.

So talk about holy cameos! Two OG reality celebrities from the OT show up. These two are legendary influencers whose legacy continues to have an impact on us to this day. And there they are, together beside Jesus, enjoying a conversation that could never have been scripted. This is beyond epic.

Suddenly, there they are: Moses, God's chosen leader who led the Israelites out of Egypt and was given the law for God's people, and Elijah, God's prophet who won the ultimate spiritual showdown with the priests of Baal, igniting a water-soaked altar sacrifice in a fiery conflagration while the pagans couldn't get a spark to sputter. Symbolically speaking, Moses represents Jewish law, the old system for relating to God, and Elijah represents Jewish prophecy, which foretold the new way—the way embodied in their midst in the form of Jesus Christ, the promised Messiah, the Son of God.

Can you imagine that scene? Jesus mingling with Moses and Elijah, talking about what's about to happen as Christ fulfills His purpose for coming to earth—to fulfill both the law and the words of the prophets. While it's a unique and perhaps surprising trio, Jesus next to Moses and Elijah reveals less of a contrast and more of a fulfillment. Because the Transfiguration, as this event is called, brings complete clarity to any and all questions left over in the old covenant.

The Transfiguration speaks to the moment when heaven proclaims to the world that Jesus is not equal to Moses or to Elijah or to any of the prophets or any of the previous kings or any of the leaders or any other person in human history.

Jesus is in a place all by Himself.

Jesus is above Moses.

Jesus is above Elijah.

Jesus is God with skin.

Jesus is the Incarnation, Immanuel, God with us in human form.

Jesus is the Savior who lived, died, was buried, and rose again.

Incomparable and Unequaled

Just as we must never overlook the essential necessity of our salvation, we must never lose sight of the fact that Jesus is not equal to anyone. He's not a good leader with some divine commandments to share like Moses. He's not a prophet sent to speak on behalf of God regarding future events. He's not a great rabbinical prodigy sent to teach the Torah. He's not a social activist who is going to overthrow the Roman occupation and restore Israel to prominence as a nation.

Jesus is the Living Son of God who saves us from all our sins.

We must stop placing Jesus on the same stage with anyone else, with cultural, political, religious, historical influencers and leaders both past and present.

Jesus is not their equal.

Jesus is above George Washington and Abraham Lincoln.

Jesus is above Joe Biden and Donald Trump.

Jesus is above Elon Musk and Mark Zuckerberg.

Jesus is above The Beatles and the Rolling Stones.

Jesus is above Johnny Cash and Dolly Parton.

Jesus is above Tom Hanks and Meryl Streep.

Jesus is above Billy Graham and Martin Luther King Jr.

Jesus is above Samuel Rodriguez or whoever your pastor may be!

Why is Jesus incomparably above everyone else? Simply put, because "there is salvation in no one else! God has given no other name under heaven by which we must be saved" (Acts 4:12 NLT). There is no one like Jesus.

So, stop placing Jesus on equal footing or on the same stage with the other important influencers in your life. Stop acting as if your faith is just a lifestyle fad that you're trying out to see if it works. Stop letting your faith run hot or cold depending on your circumstances. Stop living as if you are anyone other than a child of the King, a co-heir with Christ, an overcomer who can do all things—not just some things or even hard things but all things—through Christ who strengthens you! "By his divine power, God has given us everything we need for living a godly life. We have received all of this by coming to know him, the one who called us to himself by means of his marvelous glory and excellence" (2 Peter 1:3 NLT).

> Jesus is the Living Son of God who saves us from all our sins.

In your heart, in your mind, in your actions, it is time to elevate Jesus.

If you want to see the glory of God, make Jesus your priority.

If you want the same Spirit in you to transform you into the likeness of Jesus, keep your eyes fixed on Him. Because nothing and no one exceeds who Christ is, what He has done, and all He is doing for you at this very moment as your eyes read these words. When you make God first, you will never be last. When you lift Him up, He will lift you up. Your elevation is directly proportional to His exaltation. "Seek the Kingdom of God above all else, and live righteously, and he will give you everything you need" (Matthew 6:33 NLT).

Jesus is not equal to your family.

Jesus is not equal to your career.

Jesus is not equal to your bank account.

Jesus is not equal to your social media presence.

Jesus is not even equal to your ministry or your calling.

Jesus is not equal to Elijah or Moses or to the Law or the Prophets.

Jesus is the fulfillment, and therefore, He is above everything and everyone else.

Only Jesus is Lord.
Only Jesus is Savior.
Only Jesus can set you free.
Only Jesus can make a way where there is no way.
Only Jesus can empower you to overcome all obstacles.
Only Jesus can provide the victory of fulfilling your hope.
Only Jesus is worthy of your praise.
Only Jesus is worthy of your honor.
Only Jesus is worthy of your worship.
Only Jesus.

THE SAME SPIRIT IN YOU

This chapter points out that even when you're filled by the Holy Spirit and walking by faith, you will still encounter obstacles and be challenged by circumstances. Whether your oven catches fire, your car breaks down, your body struggles to recover from disease, or your relationship with a loved one disappoints you, you still have victory. God has gone before you and His Spirit dwells in you. Those momentary and light afflictions you suffer help you grow stronger as you persevere in your faith. They build hope, a hope that is victorious and never goes unfulfilled.

Use the questions below to help you see with the eyes of your heart the victory that Christ has secured through your salvation. Then, after taking a deep breath and calming your heart before the Lord, spend a few minutes in prayer. Open your heart to the joy of your salvation. Claim the victory that is already yours thanks to what your incomparable Savior, Jesus Christ, has done for you.

1. When have you recently experienced God's protection or provision? How did the Spirit within you prepare you and reassure you of God's imminent faithfulness?

2. What comes to mind when you consider the victory you have because of your salvation? What are some areas where you're relying on the eyes of your heart to sustain faith in the victory God will soon reveal?

3. What stands out or resonates most for you in the scene of the Transfiguration? What does this scene reveal about who Jesus is and what He's done in your life?

———————— **PRAYER** ————————

Dear God, forgive me for the times I have lost sight of Your promises and dwelt on my problems instead. Thank You for going before me and making a way where I cannot see one, for providing for all my needs, and for protecting me from danger. I give You thanks and praise for the victory I have in Christ and for the free gift of salvation through His sacrifice on the cross. As I become more attuned to the same Spirit that raised Jesus from the dead within me, give me ears to hear, Lord, and open the eyes of my heart so that I can hear and see You everywhere I go. In Jesus' name, Amen.

PART 3

HAND

Imparted by the Spirit

If we live by the Spirit, let us also keep
in step with the Spirit.

Galatians 5:25 ESV

8

ONE TOUCH

Healing in the Same Spirit

God promises healing for His children—if He did it before, He will do it again!

Through the power of the Holy Spirit, healing is always possible in the name of Jesus.

As a lifelong runner, I've consistently enjoyed numerous health benefits from my favorite form of cardiovascular exercise. Not only is running good for my heart, but it also strengthens my respiratory, circulatory, and nervous systems. My legs, calves, quads, and glutes have developed muscles and grown stronger. My brain gets more oxygen along with nutrients that boost mental functioning. And I'm rewarded with endorphins that elevate mood and alleviate stress throughout my body.

I'm not alone in enjoying these benefits. According to recent data, around fifty million Americans run or jog at least once each week.[1] Like me, some runners enjoy it simply because they like doing it and have continued running since they were young. Others choose to run for the aforementioned health benefits as well as to burn calories and lose weight. Some run simply for the boost to their mood and mental health, relieving stress and enjoying the all-natural runner's high.

Whatever the reason someone runs, doctors and medical experts agree that it's one of the best ways to achieve and sustain good health. "If running or exercise were a pill," says Dr. Todd Buckingham, PhD, an exercise physiologist and proponent of running, "it would be the most widely prescribed drug in the world for all the benefits for your health that it has. . . . Running is medicine."[2]

The older I get, however, the more I've seen an increase in the injuries and ailments that plague most runners at some point. One of the most common is known as "runner's knee," or Patellofemoral syndrome if you're in the doctor's office.[3] Triggered and aggravated by overuse, runner's knee may result from cartilage wearing down and becoming thinner. Pushing through the pain to keep running often compounds the problem by shifting the kneecap out of alignment.

After resting, icing, heating, and using Ibuprofen to heal my sore knee for a few weeks, I finally went to my primary care physician and explained my problem. He laid out my options for recovery, which I heard as a binary choice: either abstain from running for at least four to six weeks or allow him to inject a prescription steroid into the cartilage area of my afflicted knee.

I feel no shame in telling you that I took the quick and easy option and got the shot. Within 24 hours, my pain had subsided almost completely. Within 48 hours, I went on a slow jog through our neighborhood with a smile on my face. On my run that afternoon, I reflected on how supernatural healing (all healing is supernatural) tends to work the same way.

Some healing requires a process of gradual improvement over time, often doing what has been prescribed or what the Holy Spirit has instructed you to do or both. Sometimes, though, healing can be immediate, instantaneous, and ineffable. The pain or malady seems to command all your attention, and then suddenly it stops. Stunned and disoriented at first, you recognize the old familiar sensation of inhabiting your body pain-free.

Because sometimes healing only takes one touch.

Holy Healing

We live in a broken world filled with broken people. Broken families, broken children, and broken generations. Nations are broken, cities are broken, communities are broken. We are broken physically, mentally, spiritually, relationally, and financially. When we stop and look around us, we witness a broken world that is on life support, sick and gasping for breath, wounded and bleeding out.

Broken by sin, we're wounded by words as well as sickened by silence. We carry secrets that manifest in our bodies as the weight of our burdens crushes our minds, hearts, and spirits. Wounded people bleed on and injure others—often those people they love the most. Broken people break people, hurting people hurt people, and traumatized people traumatize people.

Not only does our God save, our God heals!

But here is God's promise, the word of the Lord given to His people thousands of years ago and still just as timeless and relevant today: "Salvation will come like the dawn, and your wounds will quickly heal. Your godliness will lead you forward, and the glory of the LORD will protect you from behind" (Isaiah 58:8 NLT). In the previous chapter, we looked at the victory of salvation promised by this verse, but we would be remiss not to embrace another key tenet of its truth, "Your wounds will quickly heal."

In other words, not only does our God save, our God heals.

Why is our God a healing God? Just as He saves because He is a saving God, He heals because healing is who He is and what He does. Throughout the course of human history, we bear witness to how time and time again, in each life and lifetime, from Gen A to Gen Z, God heals.

If it's lost, God will save it.

If it's broken, God will fix it.

If it's sick, God will heal it.

If it's wrong, God will make it right.

Healing is an essential aspect of who God is, and we see this reflected in one of the names by which He is known. One of the great titles and divine descriptors attributed to the almighty Creator of the universe is nothing less than *Jehovah Rapha*, our God who heals.[4] This is not someone or a group of people assigning a name to God. This is the descriptor God attributes to Himself.

We see this title actualized after God liberated the Israelites from Egyptian captivity. They spent three days in the desert and desperately needed water. When they finally found a river, the water was contaminated and undrinkable. God instructed them to put a piece of wood in the water, which they did, and He purified the water. Yes, this was likely the first holy water!

Following this incident, they received the word of the Lord.

If you listen carefully to the LORD your God and do what is right in his eyes, if you pay attention to his commands and keep all his decrees, I will not bring on you any of the diseases I brought on the Egyptians, for I am the LORD, who heals you.

Exodus 15:26

The original Hebrew for this last supernatural sobriquet is *Jehovah Rapha*, "the Lord who heals you."[5]

God is the Great I AM—if He was the Lord who heals then, He is the Lord who heals now. If He healed the Israelites then, then He will heal you now. Your wounds will quickly heal (see Isaiah 58:8) because healing is God's promise to His children. If God did it before, He will do it again. We see this promise expressed consistently, in word and in healing deed, throughout the pages of Scripture:

Worship the LORD your God, and his blessing will be on your food and water. I will take away sickness from among you, and none will miscarry or be barren in your land. I will give you a full life span.

Exodus 23:25–26

[He] forgives all your sins and heals all your diseases.

Psalm 103:3

But because of our sins he was wounded, beaten because of the evil we did. We are healed by the punishment he suffered, made whole by the blows he received.

Isaiah 53:5 GNT

Christ himself carried our sins in his body to the cross, so that we might die to sin and live for righteousness. It is by his wounds that you have been healed.

1 Peter 2:24 GNT

Say it out loud right now: *Jehovah Rapha—the Lord who heals!*

Just One Touch

Out of the many healing experiences we find in the Bible, one stands out in reminding us that it only takes one touch. This passage illustrates the power of faith in action. Rather than waiting on God's healing touch to come to her, one desperate woman decided to find healing by touching the Lord:

A woman in the crowd had suffered for twelve years with constant bleeding. She had suffered a great deal from many doctors, and over the years she had spent everything she had to pay them, but she had gotten no better. In fact, she had gotten worse. She had heard about Jesus, so she came up behind him through the crowd and touched his robe. For she thought to herself, "If I can just touch his robe, I will be healed." Immediately the bleeding stopped, and she could feel in her body that she had been healed of her terrible condition. Jesus realized at once that healing power had gone out from him, so he turned around in the crowd and asked, "Who touched my robe?" His disciples said to him, "Look at this crowd pressing around you. How can you ask, 'Who touched me?'" But he kept on looking around to see who had done it. Then the frightened woman, trembling at the realization of what had happened to her, came and fell to her knees in front of him and told him what she had done. And he said to her, "Daughter, your faith has made you well. Go in peace. Your suffering is over."

Mark 5:25–34 NLT

Preceding this encounter in the biblical narrative, we see that Jesus was on His way to heal the daughter of Jairus, a leader in the local Jewish synagogue (see Mark 5:22). Accompanying this man to his home in order to heal his little girl, Jesus had to make His way through the crowd that had gathered. That is when this desperate and afflicted woman saw an opportunity—her only remaining option—and stepped out in faith and took it.

There are many things this woman did not have. She had lost all her resources, funding, and hope in the medical professionals of her day. We're told that "she had suffered a great deal from many doctors" (verse 26), implying that not only had they not helped this poor woman recover, they had likely contributed to further suffering. Instead of getting better, she had gotten worse. She had exhausted all possible options available to her. She had no money, no resources, no health insurance, no medical insurance, no options remaining except for one—she had faith.

She believed, "If I touch Him, I will be healed." Instead of focusing on what she didn't have, she moved forward with what she did have. She had faith that Jesus, the Messiah, the man with Jairus moving through the crowd only a few feet away from her, had the power to heal her.

There was no time to try to stop Him and explain all that she had been through. There was no opportunity to describe the ordeal of suffering she had endured for twelve long years. But there was an opportunity for her to touch Jesus, to reach out and graze her fingertips along the hem of His robe as He passed by. She only needed one touch.

How often do we become so fixated on what we don't have that we lose sight of all we have by faith?

How often do we obsess about what we lack that we overlook our greatest gift?

How often do we whine about what we need rather than praise God for what we have?

This woman's faith reminds us that it's not about what we're missing—it's about what we have. We fall into the trap of conditional thinking. "If only I had more money, then I could afford better health care. If only I knew the right specialists, then I could recover. If only I lived somewhere else, then I'd have the resources I need." No, this woman had nothing except for the one thing that matters most—faith in Jehovah Rapha!

Stop whining about what you're missing; instead, start shouting about what you have.

You have a faith that moves mountains.

You have a shout that brings down walls.

You have joy that cannot be explained.

You have a peace that passes all understanding.

You have a grace that is sufficient.

You have an anointing that destroys the yoke.

You have a gift that cannot be revoked.

You have a destiny that cannot be stopped.

You have mercies that are new every morning.

You have the strength of the Father.

You have the grace of the Son.

You have the anointing of the Holy Spirit.

The same Spirit that raised Jesus from the dead.

Clearing the Crowd

When you serve God with what you have, He will take care of what you need. Faith requires you to trust God even when you do not understand Him. When you cannot imagine what you need for healing. When no cure exists. When no known treatment works. When you've exhausted all options. When you're getting worse instead of better.

What will it take for us to experience healing by one-touch faith? When we learn that sometimes we have to break in for our breakthrough.

This woman who had been hemorrhaging for a dozen years broke through all the thoughts, feelings, memories, and pain swirling inside her. She broke through the stigma of her disease, the assaults on her reputation, and the chronic fear amplifying her pain.

Her miracle was surrounded, but her faith was unleashed.

This woman broke through the crowd of obstacles internally as well as externally.

Internally, she was surrounded by her past (twelve years of suffering), her present (she was broke), her outlook (she was getting worse). Externally, her miracle maker stood surrounded by a crowd. A crowd that due to the dogmatic stigma of her infirmity would surely reject, humiliate, and alienate her. Nevertheless, she understood that sometimes we have to go *through* in order to *get to*. We must break *into* to get *out of*. We must step out of the crowd and step into the place where we can reach out and touch God. We must clear the crowd to be near Christ.

Jesus was surrounded, which often continues to be the case today. He is surrounded by dogma, legalism, bureaucracies, human constructs, ancient philosophies, and cutting-edge ministries that impede us from touching the living power and presence of Christ. If you want to experience supernatural healing that only God can do, then you must break through all the obstacles that get in your way. You must break though the ideas, rituals, dogmas, legalism, bureaucracy, false assumptions, and mistaken interpretations that surround the person, the life, the ministry, the power, and the presence of Jesus Christ.

Once you break through, once you clear the clutter and sort the surrounding area, you not only have an opportunity to touch Jesus for healing but also have the opportunity to help others experience His healing touch. Sometimes we surround God, making it difficult for the broken, the bruised, the belittled, the bloody, or the bitter to reach Him. Rather than surround Jesus with perpetual religiosity, we can reflect His power and worship His presence. While we wait for our healing, we can help others find theirs.

We see this willingness to move beyond our own woundedness so that others may find the healing touch of Jesus in the first healing recorded in the Bible.

Then Abraham prayed to God, and God healed Abimelek, his wife and his female slaves so they could have children again, for the LORD had kept all the women in Abimelek's household from conceiving because of Abraham's wife Sarah.

Genesis 20:17–18

Pretty straightforward, right? Abraham prayed, and God healed Abimelek, along with his wife and the other women in his household.

But you may remember there's more to this story. You may recall that God had promised Abraham that he would be the father of many nations. You may recall that Abraham and his wife, Sarah, were unable to conceive for many years and tried to take matters into their own hands by having Abraham father a son, who was named Ishmael, with Sarah's Egyptian maid, Hagar.

Yet God insisted that Abraham and Sarah would conceive a son together, even as years passed and they grew old, well beyond the biological season for childbearing. And then when Abraham was one hundred years old (see Genesis 21:5), which likely puts Sarah at least in her nineties, they conceived and celebrated the birth of their son, Isaac, the fulfillment of God's promise.

> Now the LORD was gracious to Sarah as he had said, and the LORD did for Sarah what he had promised. Sarah became pregnant and bore a son to Abraham in his old age, at the very time God had promised him.
>
> Genesis 21:1–2

The sequence is no coincidence. At the end of Genesis chapter 20, we're told that Abraham prayed for God to heal Abimelech and his household. At the beginning of Genesis chapter 21, we're told that Sarah got pregnant and gave birth to the son God had promised to her and Abraham. He prayed for someone who was barren. God healed them. And then God healed Sarah's barrenness as well!

When someone else's breakthrough is as important as your own, healing will take place.

You are a conduit of God's healing touch even as you reach out for Him.

Rise Up and Reach Out

This woman was broken and yet she touched God. She went through to get to. Rather than lose hope, she found faith.

You see, we all have to go through some obstacles to get to our healing. The psalmist said, "Even when I walk through the darkest valley, I will not be afraid, for you are close beside me. Your rod and your staff protect and comfort me" (Psalm 23:4 NLT). Notice he said "when" and not "if"—"when I walk through the darkest valley."

On our journey of faith, we will each experience dark valleys that require us to keep walking by faith. But not only can God reach us when we're broken—when we're broken, we can reach Him. This broken woman broke through the crowd and reached out in faith to touch the robe of her only hope for healing.

She reminds us that you don't have to be perfect to receive God's healing or to experience His love. God uses imperfect people to advance His perfect agenda. God uses broken people who dare touch Him to heal a broken world. Our Christian faith is less about promoting the perfect and more about blessing the broken. Because God never rejects the broken. "The sacrifice you desire is a broken spirit. You will not reject a broken and repentant heart, O God" (Psalm 51:17 NLT).

The purpose of God is always greater than the brokenness of human beings. God does great things with broken vessels. He fills them with His Spirit, heals them, and uses them for His glory to advance His Kingdom. In Christ, nothing—absolutely nothing—is beyond repair. So, this broken woman broke through to get to her breakthrough.

"When she heard about Jesus, she came up behind him in the crowd and touched his cloak" (Mark 5:27). She's behind Him and reaches out to touch His robe while He wasn't looking or seeming to notice. He was on route to heal Jairus's daughter, the next generation, when this woman touched Him. God did not touch her—she touched God.

She understood that if she entered into His presence, then the power would be released. She didn't have to touch His hand or hair, His elbow or ankle. She just needed to touch the robe He was wearing. She had faith that was at least the size of a mustard seed because she believed, "If I can just touch His robe, I'll be healed!"

It's time we relied on the power of God's Spirit within us and reached out to touch God instead of sitting around waiting on Him to touch us. It's time to be so zealous about our belief that we will touch God even when He's not looking our way. It's time to be so radical and so provocative that we will cause God to look our way even when He's not looking our way.

It takes radical, circumstance-shattering, life-altering, heaven-exciting, hell-upsetting faith to break through failure, rejection, shame, hurt, and brokenness to touch Jesus! "In your presence there is fullness of joy" (Psalm 16:11 ESV).

Your praise can make God look your way.

Your faith can make God look your way.

Your love for His presence can make God look your way.

If you reach for Him, God will notice you and heal you.

God will turn His face to shine upon you and take away your suffering.

It's time to touch Him.

It's time to stand out from the crowd and touch Jesus.

Touch Him with righteousness and justice.

Touch Him with redemption and reconciliation.

Touch Him with sanctification and service.

Touch Him with John 3:16 and Matthew 25.

Touch Him with orthodoxy and orthopraxy.

Touch Him with holiness and humility.

Touch Him with the vertical and horizontal of the cross.

Touch Him with your fears, your doubts, your brokenness.

Touch Him with your pain, your paralysis, your pandemic.

Touch Him with your worries, your wonders, your weaknesses.

Touch Him with your trials, your temptations, your triumphs.

You are no longer waiting for a miracle—there's a miracle waiting for you! Rise up, reach up, raise your hands, and touch the power of Jesus. The holy fire of the Spirit ignites from your spark of faith!

Your Faith Has Made You Well

We can only imagine what this poor woman may have felt or may have been thinking when the source of her healing turned around and asked, "Who touched my clothes?" (Mark 5:30). Perhaps she wondered, "How could He have felt that? I barely touched my fingers to the hem of His garment." Maybe she was terrified and felt ashamed for taking such a brazen step. After all, she was considered unclean and would have been segregated from people if they knew about her condition.

We know she was frightened, but there's a striking detail—"trembling at the realization of what had happened to her" (Mark 5:33 NLT). Sure, she may have been afraid of the consequences of what she had done. We all have those times when we decide to ask for forgiveness afterward rather than permission beforehand. But the reason she's trembling is because she realized what had happened to her. And what had happened to her?

With one touch she was healed.

With one touch she felt no pain.

With one touch her hemorrhaging stopped.

This woman who had the courageous faith to reach out and touch the robe of Jesus also had the faithful courage to step forward, fall to her knees before Him, and tell Him what she had done. She knew she could not hide—not from the One whose power had just done what no doctor had been able to do in the past twelve years. She knew that He knew who she was and what she had done. So she did the only thing she could—she confessed and she worshiped. Only her confession was not of her sin but of her salvation.

Rather than a rebuke she might have expected, rather than rage at her audacity, rather than contempt for her previous condition, this woman received affirmation and blessing. "Daughter, your faith has made you well. Go in peace. Your suffering is over" (Mark 5:34 NLT).

Jesus addressed her as daughter.

Jesus gave her His perfect peace.

Jesus ended her suffering.

When God says your suffering is over, it's over!

This healing encounter has so much bravery, beauty, and brevity in it that we might fail to realize its context within an even greater healing event. Remember that Jairus had asked Jesus to come and heal his daughter, which was what sent them hurrying through the crowd. After experiencing His divine power being appropriated by this woman whose faith facilitated her healing, Jesus blessed her and was about to resume His route to Jairus's house to heal the Jewish leader's daughter when news arrived:

> While he was still speaking to her, messengers arrived from the home of Jairus, the leader of the synagogue. They told him, "Your daughter is dead. There's no use troubling the Teacher now."
>
> But Jesus overheard them and said to Jairus, "Don't be afraid. Just have faith."
>
> Then Jesus stopped the crowd and wouldn't let anyone go with him except Peter, James, and John (the brother of James). When they came to the home of the synagogue leader, Jesus saw much commotion and weeping and wailing. He went inside and asked, "Why all this commotion and weeping? The child isn't dead; she's only asleep."
>
> The crowd laughed at him. But he made them all leave, and he took the girl's father and mother and his three disciples into the room where the girl was lying. Holding her hand, he said to her, *"Talitha koum,"* which means "Little girl, get up!" And the girl, who was twelve years old, immediately stood up and walked around! They were overwhelmed and totally amazed. Jesus gave them strict orders not to tell anyone what had happened, and then he told them to give her something to eat.
>
> Mark 5:35–43 NLT

Jesus called the woman He had just healed *daughter* and then went to restore life to a daughter of the next generation. Jairus must have been riding the proverbial roller coaster of emotions during all this. His daughter was ill and not getting better, so he went to ask Jesus to come and heal her, to which He agreed. Then, as they're making their way through the crowd, a woman barely touched Jesus, but that touch caused Him to pause and question who had just touched Him. The woman came forward and knelt while Jesus spoke kindly to her. And just as they were about to hurry home to his daughter, Jairus received word it was too late. His precious twelve-year-old girl had died.

Or had she?

Because what was Jesus' response after overhearing this sorrowful message? "Don't be afraid. Just have faith" (Mark 5:36 NLT).

Like the woman with the issue of blood who had just been healed, Jairus faced a dilemma. He, too, found himself suddenly out of options. These messengers said his daughter had died, that it was too late and pointless for Jesus to see her. Only Jesus offered a glimmer of hope by telling Jairus not to be afraid and just have faith. Jairus had to decide who to believe—the messengers of death or the Master of life.

Jesus respected the privacy of Jairus and his family by not allowing the crowd, who were already laughing at the absurdity that this girl was not dead but sleeping, to follow them into Jairus's home. Christ knew how crowds can complicate communication and amplify exaggeration. This was a personal matter. A little girl's life was in question. Taking only three of His disciples with him, along with the girl's father and mother, Jesus entered the room where the child lay and spoke softly, "Little girl, get up!"

When God says your suffering is over, it's over!

She immediately stood up and walked around (see verse 42). Her parents must have wept for joy in their gratitude and astonishment. Jesus had healed their daughter. Others said she was dead, but Jesus said she was very much alive. She wasn't dead, merely sleeping.

Two generations, two daughters, two healings.

The God who healed the woman also healed the little girl.

And He has never stopped healing.

God is the Lord who heals, Jehovah Rapha.

His Son is the Great Physician by whose stripes we are healed.

The Holy Spirit, the power source for the resurrection, is in you.

So get ready to see your body healed.

Get ready to see your family healed.

Get ready to see your mind healed.

Get ready to see your finances healed.

Get ready to see your relationships healed.

Get ready to rise up, reach out, and experience the healing power of Jesus Christ!

One touch is all it takes.

THE SAME SPIRIT IN YOU

Healing sometimes happens instantly, and sometimes healing is a process. God's power is evident in all healing and occurs according to His perfect timing, even when we are unable to understand or grasp His goodness at work. This chapter showcases the essential role that faith plays in facilitating the healing power of Jesus Christ. The woman suffering from the affliction with blood had been in pain for twelve long years. She had placed her trust and her money in the doctors treating her only to be disappointed in the results. Instead of recovering, she lapsed into more pain and more despair. Then with one touch, she was healed.

For the distraught father, Jairus, he suffered the fear, anxiety, and sense of powerlessness that comes from loving a sick child. This Jewish leader was obviously willing to do anything—including asking a stranger reputed to be the Messiah for healing—in order to see his little girl well again. Before his tears of joy, however, Jairus faced tears of grief at the presumed loss of his daughter. Only to be astonished to see Jesus speak to her and for her to obey.

These examples remind us that healing requires faith and that it is never too late because nothing is impossible with God. Reflect on the healing needed in your life by using the questions below. Then spend some time with God in prayer, listening to the voice of the same Spirit within you.

1. When have you experienced supernatural healing in your life? Did your healing happen instantly or require a gradual process? What did you learn about God from this time?

2. Whom do you identify with most in Mark chapter 5? The woman who touched Jesus' robe? Jairus? His daughter? Someone else? Why do you identify with them?

3. What needs healing in your life right now? How can you reach out to touch God instead of waiting on Him to touch you? What is He asking you to do in faith?

PRAYER

Dear Jehovah Rapha, You are indeed the God who heals! I am so grateful for all the healing power in my life right now. Forgive me, Lord, when I grumble or complain about what I lack while failing to appreciate all I have. Thank You for Your many blessings and for the ways You meet me in my brokenness. Give me courage and boldness to step out in faith so that I can touch You and reveal Your love and healing power through my life. In Jesus' name, Amen.

9

NEW WINE

Abiding in the Same Spirit

God anoints you with His grace, glory, and the gift of the Holy
Spirit to fulfill His purpose.
  When you abide in Him, He abides in you!

As a lifelong student and lover of history, I was overwhelmed with enticing options to visit on a recent trip to Rome. Like most of Italy, Rome continues to reflect both the ancient and the modern worlds. Simply walking through any piazza, alongside designer boutiques and familiar fast-food joints, I found churches where saints were entombed, the ruins of walls from the Roman Empire, or plaques and statues that commemorated a classical battle fought there. Our guide joked that even the parking lot of a McDonald's covered ancient ground where museum-worthy artifacts lay buried.

In addition to the famous sites every pilgrim comes to see, I loved touring several of the places referenced in the Bible, including the Roman Forum, Palatine Hill, the Arch of Titus, and Mamertine Prison. These sites did not disappoint and resonated with reminders of their significance, compelling me to reread Paul's Prison Epistles, as they're often called—Ephesians, Philippians, Colossians, and Philemon. As I toured the *Carcer Tullianum*, the dungeon-like basement prison at Mamertine where Peter and Paul likely spent their last days, I recalled, "As a prisoner for the Lord, then, I urge you to live a life worthy of the calling you have received" (Ephesians 4:1).

That evening, enjoying a delicious multicourse Italian dinner served with a *Chianti Classico*, I reminded our party of Paul's admonition, "Don't be drunk with wine, because that will ruin your life. Instead, be filled with the Holy Spirit" (Ephesians 5:18 NLT). This led to a discussion of the current renaissance in craft winemaking at many Italian vineyards, often using ancient viticultural techniques—such as immersing grapes in seawater prior to fermentation.[1]

As our conversation concluded, our host asked me, "Didn't Jesus say something about making new wine?"

"Why, yes, He did," I replied, both surprised and pleased. "He said not to put new wine into old wineskins, that the old skins would burst from the pressure of the new wine fermenting and releasing carbon dioxide."

"Jesus talked about *carbon dioxide*?" our host asked.

I chuckled. "No, that's what a pastor who's also a science geek talks about!"

Universal Language

Along with many memorable moments on that trip, our conversation that night lingered in my thoughts long after returning home. I reflected on Paul's warning not to be drunk with wine but to be filled with the Holy Spirit and how it tied back to Pentecost. As the gift Jesus had promised arrived, the Holy Spirit descended on the 120 believers who had gathered in the Upper Room, leaving them filled with incendiary speech. "And everyone present was filled with the Holy Spirit and began speaking in other languages, as the Holy Spirit gave them this ability" (Acts 2:4 NLT).

Apparently, their cacophony of Spirit-filled language made a dramatic impression on those nearby who heard them. While some understood them, others assumed they were drunk.

At that time there were devout Jews from every nation living in Jerusalem. When they heard the loud noise, everyone came running, and they were bewildered to hear their own languages being spoken by the believers.

They were completely amazed. "How can this be?" they exclaimed. "These people are all from Galilee, and yet we hear them speaking in our own native languages!" . . . They stood there amazed and perplexed. "What can this mean?" they asked each other.

But others in the crowd ridiculed them, saying, "They're just drunk, that's all!"

Acts 2:5–8, 12–13 NLT

Quite divergent responses, wouldn't you say? Community members from this diverse, multinational neighborhood, representing numerous languages and cultures, heard the voices of these Spirit-filled believers—and understood the message they heard in their own native language. Just imagine a United Nations meeting where an entire delegation starts speaking at once, only to be fully understood by the vast array of international participants listening.

When we are filled by the same Spirit that descended at Pentecost, we cannot keep silent because the message of the Gospel is a universal language. In computer science, a universal language is command code understandable and transferable to all operating systems. Universal programming language can express any algorithm or computational function in ways accessible to virtually any and all other computer system languages.

Every human being has fallen short of the glory of God and needs to be saved from their sins. Only Jesus, through the sacrifice on the cross and the power of the resurrection, can provide the victory of salvation. When you are filled by the Holy Spirit, your life is lived in translation. You are an advertisement for all that God is doing in your life through the power of the Spirit. Others will notice a divine difference in your life and will hear the message you're speaking—regardless of the earthly sounds you utter.

Some people, of course, will not choose to listen or hear with spiritual ears the Gospel. The heavenly language spoken through the Holy Spirit will not make sense to them because it defies the logic of their senses. "For the message of the cross is foolishness to those who are perishing, but to us who are being saved it is the power of God" (1 Corinthians 1:18). Their hearts will be resistant and closed to the invitation extended to them by the language of the Holy Spirit.

These people will respond as others did that day at Pentecost. "But others in the crowd ridiculed them, saying, 'They're just drunk, that's all!'" (Acts 2:13 NLT). Rather than marveling at the ability to hear the message in their native language, some apparently heard only gibberish and indecipherable sounds. The only explanation they could come up with, based on earthly, mortal logic, was that these believers must be sloshed, wasted, buzzed, hammered, plastered, inebriated, and intoxicated. They assumed these Spirit-filled believers must be drunk with wine.

When you live in the power of the same Spirit, others may mistakenly assume the worst about you. They will at times ridicule you, unfollow you, troll you, and mock you. They may say that you must be drunk or high, that you must be out of your mind, that you've lost all common sense and touch with reality.

But you know the truth. You are directly in touch with the ultimate reality of the cross of Jesus Christ. Others may assume the radiance in your countenance comes from bottled spirits, but you know it's the outpouring of God's Spirit.

Present Past Perfect

With such wildly divergent reactions to the symphony of Spirit-filled sounds, Peter wasted no time clarifying the situation. He not only wanted to set the record straight about the cause of their speech, but he also wanted to take the opportunity (now that a crowd had gathered) to make a direct connection to Jewish prophecy that was being fulfilled before their very eyes:

> Then Peter stepped forward with the eleven other apostles and shouted to the crowd, "Listen carefully, all of you, fellow Jews and residents of Jerusalem! Make no mistake about this. These people are not drunk, as some of you are assuming. Nine o'clock in the morning is much too early for that. No, what you see was predicted long ago by the prophet Joel:
>
>> 'In the last days,' God says,
>>> 'I will pour out my Spirit upon all people.
>> Your sons and daughters will prophesy.
>>> Your young men will see visions,
>>> and your old men will dream dreams.
>> In those days I will pour out my Spirit
>>> even on my servants—men and women alike—
>>> and they will prophesy.
>> And I will cause wonders in the heavens above
>>> and signs on the earth below—
>>> blood and fire and clouds of smoke.
>> The sun will become dark,
>>> and the moon will turn blood red
>>> before that great and glorious day of the LORD arrives.
>> But everyone who calls on the name of the LORD
>>> will be saved.'"
>
> Acts 2:14–21 NLT

Before making the dramatic leap alluding to Jewish history from the prophet Joel, Peter spoke as straightforward as he knew how. "Hey, everyone, listen up! Let me set the record straight here. No one here has been drinking alcohol. I mean, think about it, people—it's only nine o'clock in the morning!" He appeals to what's true—no one was drunk—as well as to logic held by those around him.

Apparently, even people who liked to get drunk did not start that early.

And why does Peter quote from Joel, specifically Joel 2:28–32? To bridge the old way of following the law to the new way of grace through Jesus Christ. To emphasize that the Gospel applies to all people; therefore, God pours out the gift of His Spirit on all people—young and old, men and women, servants and masters. To point out that God is still in the business of signs and wonders. And that everyone who calls on the name of the Lord shall be saved.

In the present, Peter cites the past.

The prophecy has been fulfilled by the promise.

Jesus, who is perfect as His Father is perfect, offers you forgiveness for your sins. Present. Past. Perfect.

Just as Jesus caused a stir when He quoted from Scripture to spotlight His fulfillment of them, Peter follows this example to make the same point. "So let everyone in Israel know for certain that God has made this Jesus, whom you crucified, to be both Lord and Messiah!" (Acts 2:36 NLT). As far as sermons go, I'm not sure it gets much better than this. Obviously, Peter was filled and inspired by the Spirit, but rhetorically speaking, his appeal cuts through the defenses of those listening. "Peter's words pierced their hearts" and left them asking, "What should we do?" (Acts 2:37 NLT).

Peter had their answer.

> Each of you must repent of your sins and turn to God, and be baptized in the name of Jesus Christ for the forgiveness of your sins. Then you will receive the gift of the Holy Spirit. This promise is to you, to your children, and to those far away—all who have been called by the Lord our God.
>
> Acts 2:38–39 NLT

Repent of your sins. Turn to God. Be baptized in the name of Jesus for the forgiveness of your sins. Receive the gift of the Holy Spirit.

Peter makes it clear that this is not a possibility or perception, not speculation or wishful thinking. This is God's promise to you, to your children, and to those far away, all who have been called by God and heed His call. Just as sheep know the voice of their shepherd, you are to listen and hear what God is telling you. Your sins can be forgiven. You will receive life eternal. But wait, there's more—you will receive the free gift of the Holy Spirit!

You know how you sometimes buy a tool or gadget, such as a power tool or flashlight, and batteries are included? This way you don't have to wonder what size battery you need and make a separate purchase. When batteries are included, you are given the power source you need to immediately use what you selected.

Forgive the inadequacy of my comparison, but I trust you get the idea—the Holy Spirit is the ultimate case of batteries included. When you accept God's free gift of grace and accept the salvation Jesus secured for you, then you automatically receive the indwelling of the Spirit, the same Spirit that raised Christ from the dead, the same Spirit that descended and empowered Peter and all the believers that day at Pentecost.

Peter's message remains timeless today.

Jesus Christ is both Lord and Messiah.

And God has poured out His Spirit upon you.

New Wine, New Life

While the believers at Pentecost were not drunk with wine but filled with the Spirit, I wonder if symbolically they had tasted the new wine of Christ's blood shed for them on the cross. I wonder if Jesus was foreshadowing the filling of the Holy Spirit that His followers would know after His resurrection when He said, "And no one puts new wine into old wineskins. For the old skins would burst from the pressure, spilling the wine and ruining the skins. New wine is stored in new wineskins so that both are preserved" (Matthew 9:17 NLT).

Jesus made this statement in response to the followers of John the Baptist who asked, "Why don't your disciples fast like we do and the Pharisees do?" (Matthew 9:14 NLT). We don't know the motive behind their question, only that they had observed what they considered to be a key difference in how they lived out their faith and how the disciples of Jesus lived out their faith. Jesus gave them three comparisons in response.

First, He asked them to consider how guests at a wedding respond. Do they mourn while they're with the groom? No, there's time for that later after he's no longer with them. Next, Jesus asked them whether they would use new cloth to patch an old garment. Because when the new material shrinks in the wash and puckers up, the result would make the tear worse. And finally, He pointed out that new wine is put in new wineskins, not old ones, which would burst when the new wine released fermentation gases that would expand the old, worn wineskins.

The contrast in each example makes the same point: Do not expect something new to act like something old. Wedding guests should not behave like mourners. New cloth should be sewn on new cloth. New wine requires new wineskins.

Jesus, the Bridegroom who gives Himself in love for His Bride, the Church, was on earth in human form. The time for fasting would come later, after He was no longer with them. But when you have Him, you need to recognize the need for change. New wine requires new wineskins.

When you are filled by the Holy Spirit, you cannot expect to act as you once did.

You cannot expect to relate as you once did.
You cannot expect to love as you once did.
You cannot expect to work as you once did.
You cannot expect to play as you once did.
You cannot expect to worship as you once did.
You cannot expect to praise as you once did.

Abiding in the same Spirit that raised Jesus from the dead means a fresh start, a clean slate. You are a new creature in Christ who has been washed white as snow by the blood of the Lamb. You have a new life in the power and freedom of God's Spirit. Your life will never be the same. Abiding in the same Spirit, you accept your anointing.

What is the anointing? The anointing is heaven's authority upon your divine assignment. The anointing is God's power to fulfill His purpose. The anointing is God's presence that enables you to occupy His promises. The anointing is God's super over your natural enabling you to experience the supernatural. The anointing is God's grace and glory empowering you through the gift of the Spirit. The anointing is what happens when you abide in the Spirit.

When you abide in Him, He abides in you!

> **When you abide in Him, He abides in you!**

Anointed for More

Fresh oil, not new wine, was often used to signify the anointing of those the Lord had chosen prior to the coming of Christ. In the Old Testament, when people were anointed, they were anointed from the outside in. Someone, often God's prophet or a leader with authority, would use olive oil to smudge the forehead, or perhaps the lips or the chest over the heart, in recognition of their chosen designation. Whether a private moment between two individuals or a public ceremony viewed by countless others, an anointing was an event that tangibly demonstrated one's favor with God and man. The psalmist wrote, "Fine oils have been poured on me" (Psalm 92:10).

As with many other aspects relating to God, anointing changed when the Father sent His only Son to earth to ransom His people. Because Jesus died on the cross, was resurrected, and sent His Holy Spirit, we are no longer anointed this same way as before. Rather than from the outside in, we are anointed from the inside out. Oil on our bodies no longer designates our anointing. The Spirit within our hearts designates our anointing. "The anointing you received from him remains in you" (1 John 2:27). The implications extend far beyond the external/internal distinction.

Because you have been anointed by the Holy One, you have knowledge (see 1 John 2:20).

Because the anointing lives inside of you, greater is He that is in you than he that is in the world (see 1 John 4:4).

Because the anointing lives inside of you, out of your belly, shall flow rivers of living water (see John 7:38).

Because you are anointed by the Holy Spirit and abide in His power, God works through you to change the world.

You are anointed.

You are not a victim—you are anointed.

You are not broke, busted, and disgusted—you are anointed.

You are not the devil's sparring partner—you are anointed.

If you want to serve as a spiritual, countercultural alternative to the heartbreaking narrative of this broken world, then you are anointed to speak in the language of the Word Made Flesh, Jesus Christ. In our world today, with so many different people confused and uncertain, so many identifying with so many descriptors, so many adjectives, so many pluralities, I dare you to respond in a way that will provoke demons to flee. You are anointed to proclaim good news and set captives free:

The Spirit of the Lord is upon me, because he has anointed me to proclaim good news to the poor. He has sent me to proclaim liberty to the captives and recovering of sight to the blind, to set at liberty those who are oppressed.

Luke 4:18 ESV

Our world is full of other spirits right now—ones identified in Scripture:

The spirit of divination (see Acts 16:16–18)

The spirit of jealousy (see Galatians 5:19–20)

The spirit of deception/lying (see Revelation 12:10)

The spirit of perversion (see 2 Peter 2:14)

The spirit of heaviness (see Isaiah 61:3)

The spirit of fear (see 2 Timothy 1:7)

The spirit of death (see Matthew 10:28)

The spirit of the antichrist (see 1 John 2:18–19)

But there's only one Holy Spirit—the same Spirit that was hovering when the earth was still formless and empty (see Genesis 1:1–2).

It is the same Spirit that enabled Joshua to survive the desert, cross over the Jordan, shout down the walls of Jericho, and step into the Promised Land (see Numbers 27:18).

It is the same Spirit that came upon a shepherd boy enabling him to defeat the giant called Goliath, to conquer the city of Jerusalem, and to bring back the Ark of the Covenant (see 1 Samuel 16:13).

If you want to live out of your anointing, if you want order instead of chaos, if you want life instead of death, if you want springs of living water instead of drought, if you want to cross over your Jordan and shout down the obstacles in front of you and step into the place God has for you, if you want to bring down the giant looming in your way, then the Holy Spirit is essential!

If you want to possess your destiny, reflect God's glory, and experience the fullness of life Jesus came to bring, then your anointing in the Holy Spirit is the foundation.

The Holy Spirit is the foundation for your transformation into Christ's likeness. "Don't you know that you yourselves are God's temple and that God's Spirit dwells in your midst?" (1 Corinthians 3:16).

You are not just a human being, you are a spiritual being.

You not only occupy space, you house divinity.

You are not just another person, you are a temple of the Holy Spirit.

You are anointed for more!

From Assignment to Acceptance

Although it occurs the instant you're filled by the Holy Spirit, your anointing also evolves as you mature in your faith and grow stronger in your relationship with God. We see this clearly in the life of David, delineated in three separate but progressive stages or seasons—a season of assignment, of acceptance, and of advancement.

David received his first anointing in private, in his father's house in Bethlehem. "So Samuel took the horn of oil and anointed him in the presence of his brothers, and from that day on the Spirit of the Lord came powerfully upon David" (1 Samuel 16:13). Although David was anointed then, he had to wait to become king of Israel until God's chosen time. This meant David had to serve King Saul, the man still on the throne at that time. David experienced a season of preparation and growth prior to moving into his next season.

There is a lesson in David's example that holds true for us and our anointing: God anoints you in private before He anoints you in public. He anoints you in the presence of your family before He anoints you in the presence of your enemies. He anoints you to wait before He anoints you to win.

David gained considerable experience while he waited to move on to his next season of anointing. He did not remain passive or assume the new assignment would fall in his lap. David served the king who was still enthroned. He gained battle experience and political acumen.

He learned how to endure a powerful enemy—who just happened to be the king, the father of David's best friend, and the father of David's wife. David enjoyed deep abiding friendship with Jonathan. He lived actively, proactively, and obediently while moving from his anointing of assignment to his anointing of acceptance.

David accepted his anointing the moment Saul died. After waiting years for his turn to lead, David finally got his shot. "Then the men of Judah came to Hebron, and there they anointed David king over the tribe of Judah" (2 Samuel 2:4). He had to wait for Saul to die in order to receive his new public anointing. When certain things die, you receive a new anointing.

When unbelief dies, you receive a new anointing.

When unforgiveness dies, you receive a new anointing.

When doubt dies, you receive a new anointing.

When fear dies, you receive a new anointing.

When hatred and jealousy and bitterness and greed die, you receive a new anointing.

But praise be to God, we're living by the grace of Jesus. When certain things die, we can then more fully accept our assigned anointing. He has already anointed you with the Holy Spirit, who will make certain these things die within you, and then when they are extinguished, you will receive a fresh anointing. "May God himself, the God of peace, sanctify you through and through. May your whole spirit, soul and body be kept blameless at the coming of our Lord Jesus Christ" (1 Thessalonians 5:23).

David went from a private anointing to a public anointing. You need to realize, however, that he was anointed to be king of Judah before he was king of Israel. He received an anointing to occupy a portion of his promise before he was anointed to lead over all of the promise. Sometimes God will anoint you for a season in a portion of your promise to see if you are faithful, to see if you can manage it, to see if you have the maturity to lead with integrity. In other words, God will anoint you over Judah before He anoints you over Israel.

It is worth noting that *Judah* means praise.

So don't expect to rule over Israel until your praise rules.

As you wait to move from one season of anointing to another, as you abide in the same Spirit, show God your praise is unconditional. Your praise cannot by stifled. Let Him know that you love, worship, thank, praise, and serve Him no matter when or if you experience your next season. The same God who anoints you with the Holy Spirit will anoint you for your new season according to His perfect timing. Let your praise fuel your patience as you move into your next anointing!

Advanced Anointing

When you receive the Holy Spirit, you are anointed for your assignment, you move into acceptance, and then see it fulfilled into advancement. Once David was king over Israel, he still had lessons to learn and growth to experience, particularly regarding how he used his power and the price of yielding to temptation. "When all the elders of Israel had come to King David at Hebron, the king made a covenant with them at Hebron before the LORD, and they anointed David king over Israel" (2 Samuel 5:3).

This was his advanced anointing. He fulfilled his assignment, accepted and moved into it, then grew and advanced further.

Similarly, yet upgraded exponentially through the finished work of Jesus Christ on the cross, you are anointed with fresh oil to advance into all that the Lord has for you. When you abide in the Holy Spirit, your threefold anointing explodes with the *dunamis* power of God in ways that not only change you but change the world around you. Your anointing is when the grace, gift, and glory of God inside of you come together empowering you to experience the abundant power of heaven come to earth.

What do you do once you move into your advanced anointing?

Following the example of Jesus, you go about doing good and healing the oppressed. "How God anointed Jesus of Nazareth with the Holy Spirit and with power. He went about doing good and healing all who were oppressed by the devil, for God was with him" (Acts 10:38 ESV). You overcome evil and heal the sick. "And they cast out many demons and anointed with oil many who were sick and healed them" (Mark 6:13 ESV). You pray and anoint others. "Is anyone among you sick? Let him call for the elders of the church, and let them pray over him, anointing him with oil in the name of the Lord" (James 5:14 ESV).

From Genesis to Revelation and still today, we discover that anointed people do what others will not do. Anointed people do what others cannot do. When you abide in the power of the Spirit and live out your anointing, you speak the language of grace. Your speech, your attitude, and your actions communicate Christ in ways that some will be drawn to while others will assume that you're drunk.

> When you are anointed, you are saved, delivered, healed, and chosen.

Anointed people do not whine. Anointed people worship. Anointed people do not focus on the darkness. Anointed people turn on the light. Anointed people do not make excuses. Anointed people make history.

Under the anointing . . .

We shout down walls.

Bring down giants.

Pray down fire.

Cast out devils and demons.

Lay hands on the sick.

Speak truth with love.

Pursue righteousness.

Show our children how to pray.

Advance the Lamb's agenda.

We embrace the One who is invincible as we believe for the impossible and accomplish the incredible. We exude justice, lavish love, show mercy, and walk humbly before God.

When you are anointed, you are saved, delivered, healed, and chosen. When you are anointed, your family is anointed. When you are anointed, your dream is anointed. Your assignment is anointed. Your going in is anointed, and your going out is anointed. Your faith is anointed. Your present is anointed. Your future is anointed.

Like David, like Paul, and like Peter and the believers at Pentecost, you are anointed by the Spirit of God. You live today because you, my friend, have a God-appointed, God-orchestrated, God-ordained assignment. You are uniquely qualified for the anointing you have through the Holy Spirit.

God called you.
God chose you.
God saved you.
God delivered you.
God healed you.
Not just for you to have a testimony.
Not for you to have a title.
But for you to fulfill His assignment.

Remember, the enemy attacks you not because of the foolish things you did but because of the glorious things you are about to do. But you cannot execute your purpose, fulfill your mission, or complete your assignment without one critical element: the anointing of the Holy Spirit. To sustain and grow into the fullness of your anointing, you abide in the same Spirit.

> But the anointing that you received from him abides in you, and you have no need that anyone should teach you. But as his anointing teaches you about everything, and is true, and is no lie—just as it has taught you, abide in him.
>
> 1 John 2:27 ESV

This is the secret to abiding in your anointing and growing in it from season to season.

Without the anointing, you toil in the world of the pathetic.
With the anointing, you soar in the land of the prophetic.
Without the anointing, you fail or at best survive.
With the anointing, *you thrive*!

─────────── THE SAME SPIRIT IN YOU ───────────

Once again, use these questions and the prayer starter below as an opportunity to reflect upon and further explore your anointing in the Holy Spirit. Make these next few minutes a sacred time so that you may be attuned to the voice of the Spirit. Eliminate as many distractions and interruptions as possible. Silence your phone, shut your laptop, close your screen, and give Jesus your full and undivided attention for this time with Him. Give God thanks and praise for the anointing you have through the same Spirit that raised Jesus from the dead.

1. What stands out or resonates most for you in this chapter? Why?

2. What evidence do you see in your life for your anointing as you abide in the Holy Spirit? How has this been confirmed by what you read in this chapter?

3. When you think about the three seasons of anointing—assignment, acceptance, advancement—where are you right now? What have you been experiencing in preparation for your next season of anointing?

--- PRAYER ---

Dear Lord, I am humbled by the gift of Your anointing in the Holy Spirit and grateful for all I continue learning in this season. Give me patience to remain obedient so that I may grow in experience and be prepared when, in Your timing, I move into the next aspect of my anointing. May I rely on Your power alone in carrying out my anointing. Use me for Your purposes, God, to heal others, to overcome evil, to set captives free, and to point them to Your Son, my Lord and Savior, Jesus Christ. In Jesus' name, Amen.

10

FRESH FRUIT

Growing in the Same Spirit

The same Spirit that raised Jesus from the dead produces
spiritual fruit in you.
The fruit of the Spirit in you is the love of God in all its forms.

I'm not much of a gardener, but I love a beautiful garden.
One of my favorites is the *Jardin Botanico*, officially known as
the Botanical Garden of the University of Puerto Rico, sprawling
across nearly three hundred acres in the capital city of San Juan. The
garden originally started as a living, ongoing scientific and botanical
research center for studying native and exotic plants, trees, flowers, grasses, and the island's many bird species. Open to the public
free of charge and offering guided tours and seminars, the property
quickly grew into an urban respite for nature lovers, both residents
and visitors alike.[1]

Along its many paths, walkways, roads, and bridges, you will
find lakes, waterfalls, and modern outdoor sculpture installations
by Puerto Rican and Latin artists. The garden features an herbar-
ium flourishing with more than 36,000 specimens being studied and

researched by University of Puerto Rico researchers and students. Both seasonal exhibits and permanent collections of rare and endangered species of most tropical flora fill the landscape, including Heliconia with their red-orange blooms like tiny lobster claws.

The Orchid Garden showcases a dramatic array of the various kinds flourishing in the Tropics in almost every color. With more than 125 species of palm trees, the arboretum includes species dating back to the fifteenth century. An Aquatic Garden recreates scenes of water lilies painted by Impressionistic painter Claude Monet at his home in Giverny. There's even a secluded bamboo chapel within the bamboo forest on the grounds.

Any visitor can tell from just one visit that such diverse and distinct natural beauty did not happen by accident. The layout and arrangement of its various overlapping areas as well as the non-organic items, such as sculptures and walkways, reflect an aesthetic intentionality. While the many plants, flowers, trees, grasses, and herbs within this garden grow naturally, they require attention in order to thrive. To sustain its splendor, the *Jardin Botanico* requires a dedicated team committed to cultivating and tending its vast array of all that grows there.

Every living organism requires cultivation and intentionality in order to thrive. The same is true for the fruit of the Spirit growing in you.

The Same Tree

When you grow in the power of the Holy Spirit within you, your life will bear the fruit of the Spirit. This spiritual fruit will blossom and ripen within you simply because the same Spirit that raised Jesus from the dead resides in you. The new wine of the Spirit in you produces a new bouquet of flavors. Paul identified the fruit of the Spirit in his letter to the Galatians as "love, joy, peace, forbearance, kindness, goodness, faithfulness, gentleness and self-control" (5:22–23). These attributes reflect who God is, and since we are created in His image by Him and empowered by His Spirit within us, it makes sense that these attributes grow in us.

Although nine qualities are listed by Paul, they are collectively the fruit of the Spirit—not fruits, plural. Why? Because they all come from the same tree! Different kinds of fruits come from different kinds of trees—oranges from orange trees, pears from pear trees, figs from fig trees. All varieties of apples, however, come from apple trees. Whether Granny Smith, Gala, Honeycrisp, or Red Delicious, they are all variants within the apple family.

Similarly, these nine characteristics cited by Paul all come back to love. "The fruit produced by the Holy Spirit within you is divine love in all its varied expressions" (Galatians 5:22–23 TPT). This divine love of the Spirit takes root in us because of who Jesus is and what He did on the cross. Jesus told us:

> I am the true vine, and my Father is the gardener. He cuts off every branch in me that bears no fruit, while every branch that does bear fruit he prunes so that it will be even more fruitful. You are already clean because of the word I have spoken to you. Remain in me, as I also remain in you. No branch can bear fruit by itself; it must remain in the vine. Neither can you bear fruit unless you remain in me.
>
> I am the vine; you are the branches. If you remain in me and I in you, you will bear much fruit; apart from me you can do nothing. If you do not remain in me, you are like a branch that is thrown away and withers; such branches are picked up, thrown into the fire and burned. If you remain in me and my words remain in you, ask whatever you wish, and it will be done for you. This is to my Father's glory, that you bear much fruit, showing yourselves to be my disciples.
>
> John 15:1–8

How do we produce the fruit of the Spirit? By abiding in Christ! We cannot bear fruit by ourselves. Just as a branch cut off from its tree trunk cannot produce fruit and will die, we do not have the power to grow spiritual fruit in our own ability. Left to our own attempts, we fail, we die, we remain cut off from God. We become like the branch Jesus mentions that withers, dies, and gets tossed into the fire to clear the ground.

When we remain in Jesus and He remains in us through the indwelling of the Holy Spirit, we bear much fruit. When we abide in Christ and nourish our faith with His words, God's truth, we grow more mature and produce divine fruit—love, joy, peace, patience, kindness, goodness, faithfulness, gentleness, and self-control. When you live in your anointing and obey God into the next season of your anointing, your fruit ripens.

When we remain in Jesus and He remains in us through the indwelling of the Holy Spirit, we bear much fruit.

Divine love takes root in your soul and blossoms in your thoughts, your words, your attitudes, and actions.

You don't rely on circumstances, money, or other people to make you happy because you have the joy of heaven growing inside you.

You don't get anxious and depressed by overwhelming demands and the noise of a chaotic world consuming you because you have peace that passes understanding.

You don't have to fight to be first, step on the backs of others to advance, or exploit opportunities for advancement because you have faith-fueled patience to trust God's timing.

You don't have to compete, compare, envy, or covet others—on social media, in your neighborhood, at church—because divine compassion blooms from God's kindness in you.

You don't have to work harder to pursue perfection or be a better person because your goodness comes from the ultimate source— God's goodness and generosity.

You don't have to force yourself to participate in church, tithe and make offerings, praise and worship, confess and forgive because your faithfulness comes from the Holy Spirit in you.

You don't have to soften your strength or dial down your divine anointing because gentleness characterizes everything you say and do.

You don't beat yourself up when you stumble or yield to temptation because your sins have been forgiven and the Holy Spirit is your strength.

This is the fruit of the Spirit growing in you.

Positive Power of Pruning

If you don't remain grounded in the truth of God's Word, if you allow weeds of temptation to distract your cultivation of spiritual fruit, if you choose to disobey God and rely on your own abilities, then you will not harvest spiritual fruit. Jesus says that the Father cuts off those branches that do not bear fruit—and prunes those who are fruitful to produce even more.

Sometimes when you don't see evidence of spiritual fruit in your life, you may be tempted to grow discouraged. As you face trials and run up against obstacles, you might feel as if all the love, patience, and kindness you have on hand gets consumed quickly by the ravenous, seemingly insatiable appetites of everyone around you. As you struggle and encounter painful disappointments and devastating losses, you might feel as though your goodness and faithfulness are withering on the vine. As you suffer injustice and inequity and labor to overcome the assumptions and expectations of others, your gentleness and self-control may rot into mush.

During these times you may tilt toward working harder in your own power to produce spiritual fruit—which we know does not work. Or, you may be inclined to neglect your soul's garden, your relationship with God, altogether and allow weeds, thorns, and pests to invade your life. But Jesus tells us that we must not lose heart when we experience hardships, which I like to think of as spiritual growing pains, because our Father prunes us to bear more fruit.

If you have any experience gardening, then you know that pruning is not simply optional but essential for plants, flowers, shrubs, and trees to thrive. Pruning removes misshapen branches that might create an imbalance and uproot the tree. Pruning removes dead blossoms so that new buds can take their place. Pruning removes diseased fruit to prevent it from spreading.

As difficult as it can be to experience at times, pruning is part of the process of our promise. Why do parents discipline their children? To hurt them or be spiteful to them? To demonstrate their supreme power and authority over them? To control and contain them to prove a point? No! Parents discipline their children because they love them and want them to grow and flourish.

Jesus made a similar comparison.

> Which of you fathers, if your son asks for a fish, will give him a snake instead? Or if he asks for an egg, will give him a scorpion? If you then, though you are evil, know how to give good gifts to your children, how much more will your Father in heaven give the Holy Spirit to those who ask him!
>
> Luke 11:11–13

In other words, what if our pruning is actually a necessary gift, allowing us to grow stronger and more fruitful? Sometimes when we want to experience more of the Spirit's power, pruning is part of the process. "My child, don't reject the LORD's discipline, and don't be upset when he corrects you. For the LORD corrects those he loves, just as a father corrects a child in whom he delights" (Proverbs 3:11–12 NLT).

Sometimes what gets pruned is something we did not need like we assumed.

Sometimes what gets pruned forces us to rely on the power of God's Spirit rather than ourselves.

Sometimes what gets pruned frees up resources required for our next season of anointing.

Sometimes what gets pruned cultivates the kind of spiritual fruit we're lacking.

Don't overlook the positive power of pruning amidst its pain.

Spiritually Fruity

When I think about spiritually fruity people in Scripture, I think of Peter. The spiritual growth and maturity evident in Peter on Pentecost reflects fruit that had already been planted by Jesus, after His resurrection but before His ascension. After denying even *knowing* Jesus—not once, not twice, but three times—even after Jesus told Peter this is what he would do, Peter might have seemed the least likely to get up and preach with such power. But there he was, jumping in and addressing the crowd that gathered within moments of receiving the Holy Spirit.

You'll recall that after the Holy Spirit descended on Peter and the other believers in the Upper Room, they began speaking the language of grace in a multitude of languages (see Acts 2:4). Jews from many other countries came running, astounded to hear their native tongue being spoken. Others, however, assumed their clamor increased in volume because they were drunk—at nine o'clock in the morning.

Peter immediately made it clear that they were not drunk, and then he demonstrated what it means to be filled with the Spirit and bear fruit. He began to preach and to pierce the hearts of those listening with the sharp edge of the Gospel of Jesus Christ. "Repent and be baptized every one of you in the name of Jesus Christ for the forgiveness of your sins, and you will receive the gift of the Holy Spirit" (Acts 2:38 ESV).

For a humble fisherman who tended to jump to conclusions and fly off the handle, Peter preached the first sermon on Pentecost with power, authority, passion, and eloquence. We're told, "And with many other words he bore witness and continued to exhort them. . . . So those who received his word were baptized, and there were added that day about three thousand souls" (Acts 2:40–41 ESV). Peter's words reflected the power of the same Spirit that raised Christ from the dead breathing new life into the crowd that had gathered.

In order to grow, virtually every living thing needs air or some form of oxygen. We see how the breath of the Spirit ignited the sparks of Peter's speech to enflame the hearts of those listening. But this is not the first time the Spirit has been described this way.

In Genesis, when God breathed life into His human creations, the Hebrew word used is *ruach*, which conveys more than just breath but energy, creativity, life, and productivity (see Genesis 1:2). With every breath we take during our life on earth, we are continually reminded how our Creator has breathed life into us. In other places in the Old Testament, such as Leviticus 26:11 and Isaiah 30:1, the original *ruach* gets translated as God's "Spirit" or "Soul" but also expresses the Lord's power, force, authority, and holiness.

In the original Greek language of the New Testament, and what we usually find here in Acts to describe the Holy Spirit, is *Pneuma*, connoting breath and wind. You'll recall that the arrival of the Spirit in the Upper Room included the loud rushing of a mighty wind (see Acts 2:2). The two words, *ruach* and *Pneuma*, both convey similar yet distinct aspects of God's Spirit, which then fills us with the same power, force, and life-giving energy that exists within the Trinity outside of chronological time and human existence.

So the breath of the Spirit fills Peter, whose literal breath becomes Spirit-inspired speech heard, we know, by at least three thousand people—the number of souls saved that day. While the Spirit certainly empowered and inspired Peter, he still actively participated by his willingness to preach and use the anointing placed on him by his Master only a few short weeks before. He was not held back by his previous failure. He did not allow shame to subvert the calling placed on his life. He was not afraid to stand up and declare that the name of Jesus Christ saves souls after having denied even knowing Him only a couple of months before then.

What made the difference?

Breakfast on the beach!

Before and After

The gospel of John describes how this divinely appointed breakfast on the beach began as a fishing trip. Peter said, "I'm going fishing," and Thomas, Nathaniel, James, and John (sons of Zebedee), and two other disciples evidently agreed to go along (see John 21:1–3). Out on the water all night, they caught nothing. Then just as dawn began to break, they glimpsed a figure on shore who called out, "Fellows, have you caught any fish?" (John 21:5 NLT).

When they replied that they had not, their inquisitor said, "Throw out your net on the right-hand side of the boat, and you'll get some!" (verse 6 NLT). When they did just as suggested, "they couldn't haul in the net because there were so many fish in it" (verse 6 NLT). That's when one of them realized this was not any random stranger strolling along at dawn.

> Then the disciple whom Jesus loved said to Peter, "It's the Lord!" When Peter heard him say that, he quickly wrapped his outer garment around him, and because he was athletic, he dove right into the lake to go to Jesus! The other disciples then brought the boat to shore, dragging their catch of fish. They weren't far from land, only about a hundred meters. And when they got to shore, they noticed a charcoal fire with some roasted fish and bread. Then Jesus said, "Bring some of the fish you just caught."
>
> So Peter waded into the water and helped pull the net to shore. It was full of many large fish, exactly one hundred and fifty-three, but even with so many fish, the net was not torn.
>
> "Come, let's have some breakfast," Jesus said to them.
>
> And not one of the disciples needed to ask who it was, because every one of them knew it was the Lord. Then Jesus came close to them and served them the bread and the fish. This was the third time Jesus appeared to his disciples after his resurrection.
>
> John 21:7–14 TPT

While John was the first to identify the person on shore as the risen Lord, Peter was the first in the water. He couldn't wait on the current, their oars, or the boat—Peter dove into the water! Remember a different scene on a lake when Peter was in a boat? There was a mighty storm raging, and once again the disciples did not recognize Jesus at first. Because He was walking on water, they thought He was a ghost (see Matthew 14:26). Peter wanted proof. "'Lord, if it's you,' Peter replied, 'tell me to come to you on the water'" (verse 28).

Jesus told Peter to come to Him, so the uncertain disciple got out of the boat and walked on water toward Jesus. Then, taking his eyes off Jesus and seeing the wind on the water, Peter started to sink and cried out for his Lord to save him (see verse 30). "Immediately Jesus reached out his hand and caught him. 'You of little faith,' he said, 'why did you doubt?'" (verse 31).

In John 21, rather than question whether it was really Jesus, instead of wanting proof, Peter didn't hesitate and jumped in the water. He didn't need to walk on it because he didn't need proof. Jesus had risen from the grave—providing more than enough proof for anyone at any time. Faith makes you walk, but forgiveness makes you jump in.

Once ashore, Peter helped his friends drag in the heavy, overfilled fishing net. And then we see a curious detail—we're told exactly how many fish they caught, 153. Knowing that nothing is coincidental in the Spirit-inspired Word of God, why would this number be significant? Could it be to emphasize the Peter we see before and after the resurrection?

Faith makes you walk, but forgiveness makes you jump in.

Let's see. The last time Peter was referenced with any association to a number was the prophetic utterance of Jesus prior to His arrest and crucifixion. "'Truly I tell you,' Jesus answered, 'this very night, before the rooster crows, you will disown me three times'" (Matthew 26:34). Yet here is his catch—153 fish, the result of obeying the instruction to try again by casting on the right-hand side. If my math skills hold up, 153 is more than 50 times the 3 denials.

Any doubts Peter may have harbored about Jesus' response to him and his disappointing fulfillment of the prophetic declaration that said Peter would adamantly deny Jesus must have vanished. Peter no longer needs proof, no longer needs to walk on water. Peter knew he was forgiven. He knew because Christ had done exactly what He had promised to do—die on the cross and rise again from the tomb.

Peter apparently, however, needed to be reminded of his anointing. Because after they had eaten a breakfast of fire-baked fish and bread, Jesus asked Peter three times, "Do you love Me?" After Peter answered, "Yes, Lord!" three times—again, no coincidence in the number—Jesus told him, "Feed My sheep" (see John 21:15–17).

Basically, Jesus emphasized to Peter that his anointing had not changed. Nor had the mission Christ had given him during their ministry together.

> And I tell you, you are Peter, and on this rock I will build my church, and the gates of hell shall not prevail against it. I will give you the keys of the kingdom of heaven, and whatever you bind on earth shall be bound in heaven, and whatever you loose on earth shall be loosed in heaven.
>
> Matthew 16:18–19 ESV

We have to wonder if these words of Jesus and the memory of their beachside brunch conversation came to mind that Day of Pentecost when Peter stood preaching before thousands of people. Filled with the power of the same Spirit that raised his Master from the dead, Peter was not the same scared, uncertain, sinking man in a storm from a few years earlier. Nor was he the impulsive man quick to react—cutting off a soldier's ear to defend Jesus in Gethsemane and then denying that he had ever met Jesus.

Peter had grown in his faith, and now the Spirit was producing fruit.

Fresh Oil, Holy Fire, New Wine

Net Working

The breakfast Jesus had with Peter and the other disciples reminds us never to lose sight of our anointed purpose. But it also illustrates how we must rely on one another if we are to grow in our faith and produce spiritual fruit. That morning they could not catch fish—until Jesus showed up. When they obeyed His instruction, they could barely lift those 153 straining their net.

This scene parallels the first time these fishermen encountered Jesus. Approximately three-plus years earlier, they had also fished all night and failed to catch anything. Jesus told them to cast their net again, which they did, and their huge catch ripped their net (see Luke 5:6). At that time Christ called them to follow Him and become fishers of men. Now, with His time on earth almost completed, Jesus has told them once again to persist and see what they catch. They have a similar huge haul—only this time their net holds. It was strained and stretched but did not break.

Dragging the full-to-capacity fishing net ashore required all of them. Peter alone could not have pulled it in, nor could any of the others. In order to fulfill your divine destiny, you will need help. Don't fool yourself into thinking you can do it without depending on other Spirit-filled believers. Drag it if you must, but do not leave your breakthrough behind.

Sometimes, the battle is to make you abandon the catch. The enemy's strategy is to overwhelm you in order to provoke you to abandon the harvest. And the enemy loves to make you feel isolated, alone, unnoticed, and unseen. So we try to drag the net all by ourselves, trying to convince ourselves we are sufficiently strong enough to haul it all by ourselves. But our life journey of faith was never meant to be traveled in solitude.

From Adam and Eve in the Garden to Jesus Christ commissioning the apostles two-by-two, partnerships enable us to fulfill our purpose. In fact, in order to grow in your anointing, you must learn to partner. Kingdom collaboration is a pre-requisite for Kingdom advancement. If you want to cultivate the fruit of the Spirit within you, then you need someone to help you weed out temptations and nourish your soul with encouragement. You need to find someone willing to challenge you, support you, pray for you, and come alongside you no matter life's circumstances.

You need to find someone who believes in you when you do not believe in yourself.

You need someone who will pray you out of your pit and praise with you in the palace.

Someone who will tell you no when your flesh tells you yes.

Someone who will push you toward your future and protect you from your past.

Someone who will speak prophetically into your destiny while rebuking the drama in your life.

Someone who will pray with you in the drought and dance with you in the rain.

Someone who, like Silas with Paul, will sing with you even when you're chained up behind closed doors.

Someone like Jonathan with David who will love you and protect you more than a brother.

Someone like Elijah with Elisha who will walk with you, mentor you, and pass on his mantle.

Someone like Ruth with Naomi who will go where you go and never abandon you.

As you abide and grow in the same Spirit, you will discover the power of partnerships with someone willing to praise with you pray with you. Jesus told us that we experience His presence in our midst and amplify our prayers to heaven when we gather with others. "Again I say to you, if two of you agree on earth about anything they ask, it will be done for them by my Father in heaven. For where two or three are gathered in my name, there am I among them" (Matthew 18:19–20 ESV).

There comes a time as you mature in your faith and get closer to a season of advancement in your anointing that God will remove dream killers and replace them with dream weavers. When you are experiencing spiritual growing pains, one of the most important prayers that you can make is asking God to remove the wrong people from your life and to bring the right people into your life. Trust that God will surround you with people who will help you drag your net.

Do you trust God for everything? Can God trust you with anything?

Keep in mind, however, that not everyone should have access to your net. Some people can handle you with an empty net, but they can't handle you with a full net.

Some people can be with you when you're broken and busted, but they can't handle you when you're blessed and favored.

Some people want you to depend on them in perpetuity, and they get high off your dependency because of your validation of them and their value. Rather than relying on the Holy Spirit, rather than living from the center of their identity in Christ, they look to you, to other people. That's why you need people who are with you both when the net is empty and when the net is full.

Not everyone should have access to your net.
If you can't be happy for me, get off my net.
If you can't celebrate with me, get off my net.
If you can't rejoice with me, get off my net.
If you can't dance with me, get off my net.
If you can't grow with me, get off my net.

When considering when and whom to trust, first ask yourself two other questions: Do you trust God for everything? Can God trust you with anything?

Once you can affirmatively and confidently answer these two, then you are ready to ask, "Whom can I trust?"

As you grow in the Spirit, you will also grow in wisdom and discernment. You will be more attuned to the voice of God and, therefore, a better spiritual listener. You will know you cannot grow into the fullness of all God has for you without other people, key partnerships, and a Spirit-filled community of believers. You will trust that God will show you whom you can trust.

He Who Is in You

On Pentecost, Peter experienced what it meant to be a fisher of men. From dragging in a net literally bursting at the seams to three years later dragging in another net that held together, Peter witnessed more than three thousand people accept Jesus and receive the gift of the Holy Spirit. He would spend the rest of his life preaching the Gospel and discipling other believers before dying a martyr's death for his faith. Peter was assigned his anointing from Jesus, accepted it fully at Pentecost, and fulfilled its advancement by being the fisher of men that Jesus called him to be.

Peter's life produced the fruit of the Spirit because he walked by faith.

Peter's life produced fruit because the same Spirit that raised Jesus from the dead was in him. The same is true for every believer who has accepted the free gift of grace and been born again. The same is true for you, my friend.

"The Spirit of God, who raised Jesus from the dead, lives in you" (Romans 8:11 NLT).

Who lives in you? The same Spirit!

Who is the Holy Spirit?

The Holy Spirit is the Third Person of the Godhead.

The Holy Spirit is the paraclete, the advocate, the counselor, the helper.

The Holy Spirit is the *pneuma*, the wind.

The Holy Spirit is the *ruach*, the breath.

The Holy Spirit is the comforter.

The Holy Spirit is the seal.

The Holy Spirit is the most powerful influencer on earth today.

The Holy Spirit is the occupant of your body and the facilitator of your destiny.

The Holy Spirit is your GPS who guides you.

The Holy Spirit is your new wine, one that Napa can't even come close to vinting.

The Holy Spirit is your best friend.

The Holy Spirit is your prayer partner.

The Holy Spirit is the most powerful, loving, transformative, innovative, creative person and force on planet earth today.

And He lives inside of *you*.

He who is in you is stronger than he who is in the world.

You are anointed by fresh oil for a divine purpose.

You are equipped for a divine destiny.

You are empowered by holy fire for a divine discovery.

You can do all things through Christ who strengthens you.

You are refreshed by new wine for a divine distinction.

You are an overcomer who has the victory of salvation.

You are a healer, a peacemaker, a prayer warrior, and a servant leader.

You are a temple of the Spirit of God.

You are a bearer of the fruit of the Spirit.

Now is your time to experience the fullness of life in the same Spirit!

THE SAME SPIRIT IN YOU

As you conclude your exploration about the power of the same Spirit in you within these pages, remember that your relationship with the Holy Spirit never ends. To help you consider what you want to take away from this chapter, and from this book as a whole, use the questions below to facilitate a time of review and reflection. Consider how you knew the Holy Spirit before you started reading this book compared to how you relate to Him now.

Spend some time in prayer and ask God to reveal your next steps of obedience as you more fully embrace your anointing and bear spiritual fruit. Praise and worship Him for all you're learning and for how He will continue to use these truths to ripen your soul.

1. How would you describe your relationship with the Holy Spirit prior to reading this book? What's the biggest change in your relationship with God's Spirit now?

2. Which of the many attributes and descriptors of the Holy Spirit stand out most to you? What do you need most from the same Spirit right now in your life?

3. What changes will you make in your life in order to cultivate more spiritual fruit? Which fruit of the Spirit do you believe needs the most attention right now? Why?

—————————————— PRAYER ——————————————

Dear Holy Spirit, thank You for all the ways You love, encourage, comfort, support, sustain, and empower me in my life. Your anointing gives me purpose and direction. Attune my heart to Your voice so that I may continue to grow, serve, love, and bear all the fruit of Your presence in my life. Grant me patience, Lord, to trust Your timing and never to rush ahead or lag behind You. I praise Your name and give You all my thanks for living in me, setting me free, and empowering me with Your life-giving resurrection power. Continue to teach me and speak to my heart about all I've learned in these pages. In Jesus' name, Amen.

NOTES

Chapter 2 Holy Dynamite

1. Nils Ringertz, "Alfred Nobel—His Life and Work," The Nobel Prize, accessed January 29, 2024, https://www.nobelprize.org/alfred-nobel/alfred-nobel-his-life-and-work.

Chapter 3 Emancipation Proclamation

1. *Merriam-Webster.com Dictionary*, s.v. "freedom," accessed January 29, 2024, https://www.merriam-webster.com/dictionary/freedom.
2. "Lincoln's Second Inaugural Address," National Parks Service, April 18, 2020, https://www.nps.gov/linc/learn/historyculture/lincoln-second-inaugural.htm.
3. "Read Martin Luther King Jr.'s 'I Have a Dream' Speech in its Entirety," NPR, January 16, 2023, https://www.npr.org/2010/01/18/122701268/i-have-a-dream-speech-in-its-entirety.

Chapter 4 Bilingual Benefits

1. Avery Hurt, "How Learning a Language Changes Your Brain," *Discover*, May 5, 2021, https://www.discovermagazine.com/mind/how-learning-a-language-changes-your-brain.
2. Hurt, "How Learning a Language Changes Your Brain."
3. Steven Leveen, "The Surprising Truth about American Bilingualism: What the Data Tells Us," America the Bilingual, accessed January 29, 2024, https://www.americathebilingual.com/the-surprising-truth-about-american-bilingualism-what-the-data-tells-us.
4. Hurt, "How Learning a Language Changes Your Brain."

Chapter 5 A New Song

1. Ethan Millman, "Latin Music Revenue Surpasses $1 Billion in U.S. For First Time," *Rolling Stone*, April 12, 2023, https://www.rollingstone.com/music/music -latin/latin-music-us-revenue-1-billion-1234713141.
2. Millman, "Latin Music Revenue Surpasses $1 Billion."
3. J. John Canon, "Pentecost," CanonJJohn.com, accessed January 29, 2024, https://canonjjohn.com/2023/05/27/pentecost.

Chapter 6 A Fearless Heart

1. Timothy Keller, "Shalom," TheNIVBible.com, accessed January 29, 2024, https://www.thenivbible.com/blog/meaning-shalom-bible.
2. Sara Barnes, "This Is How a Crowd in Argentina Reunited a Lost Boy With His Dad," My Modern Met, August 30, 2022, https://mymodernmet.com/lost -child-argentina.

Chapter 8 One Touch

1. "Running and Jogging Statistics and Facts," Statista, September 14, 2023, https://www.statista.com/topics/1743/running-and-jogging.
2. Jenessa Connor, "When You Run Every Day," *Runner's World*, June 15, 2022, https://www.runnersworld.com/training/a40292294/benefits-of-running-every-day.
3. Hedy Marks, "10 Common Running Injuries: Prevention and Treatment," WebMD, June 9, 2022, https://www.webmd.com/fitness-exercise/running-injuries -causes-prevention-treatment.
4. Hope Bolinger, "Why Do We Call on God as 'Jehovah Rapha' for Healing?," CrossWalk.com, May 25, 2021, https://www.crosswalk.com/faith/bible-study/why -do-we-call-on-god-as-jehovah-rapha-for-healing.html.
5. Frank Santora, "Why Should We Know God as 'Jehovah Rapha'?," Bible Study Tools, December 20, 2022, https://www.biblestudytools.com/bible-study /topical-studies/why-should-we-know-god-as-jehovah-rapha.html.

Chapter 9 New Wine

1. Julia Eskins, "Ancient Wines Are Having a Moment in Italy. Here's Why," *National Geographic*, July 6, 2021, https://www.nationalgeographic.com/travel /article/ancient-wines-are-having-a-moment-in-italy-heres-why.

Chapter 10 Fresh Fruit

1. "Universidad de Puerto Rico," University of Puerto Rico, accessed January 29, 2024, https://www.upr.edu/jardin-botanico.

SAMUEL RODRIGUEZ is president of the National Hispanic Christian Leadership Conference (NHCLC), the world's largest Hispanic Christian organization, with more than 42,000 U.S. churches and many additional churches spread throughout the Spanish-speaking diaspora.

Rodriguez stands recognized by CNN, Fox News, Univision, and Telemundo as America's most influential Latino/Hispanic faith leader. *Charisma* magazine named him one of the forty leaders who changed the world. The *Wall Street Journal* named him one of the top twelve Latino leaders, and he was the only faith leader on that list. He has been named among the "Top 100 Christian Leaders in America" (*Newsmax* 2018) and nominated as one of the "100 Most Influential People in the World" (*Time* 2013). Rodriguez is regularly featured on CNN, Fox News, Univision, PBS, *Christianity Today*, the *New York Times*, the *Wall Street Journal*, and many others.

Rodriguez was the first Latino to deliver the keynote address at the annual Martin Luther King Jr. Commemorative Service at Ebenezer Baptist Church, and he is a recipient of the Martin Luther King Jr. Leadership Award presented by the Congress of Racial Equality.

Rodriguez advised former American presidents Bush, Obama, and Trump, and he frequently consults with Congress regarding advancing immigration and criminal justice reform as well as religious freedom and pro-life initiatives. By the grace of God, the Rev. Samuel Rodriguez is one of the few individuals to have participated in the inauguration ceremonies of two different presidents representing both political parties.

In January 2009, Pastor Sam read from the gospel of Luke for Mr. Obama's inaugural morning service at Saint John's Episcopal

Church. On January 20, 2017, at Mr. Trump's inauguration, with more than one billion people watching from around the world, Pastor Sam became the first Latino evangelical to participate in a U.S. presidential inaugural ceremony, reading from Matthew 5 and concluding with "in Jesus' name!" In April 2020, Reverend Rodriguez was appointed to the National Coronavirus Recovery Commission to offer specialized experience and expertise in crisis mitigation and recovery to help national, state, and local leaders guide America through the COVID-19 pandemic.

Rodriguez is the executive producer of two films: *Breakthrough*, the GMA Dove Award winner for Inspirational Film of the Year, with an Academy Award nomination for Best Original Song, and *Flamin' Hot*, in partnership with Franklin Entertainment and 20th Century Fox. He is also co-founder of TBN Salsa, an international Christian-based broadcast television network, and he is the author of *You Are Next*, *Shake Free*, *Be Light*—a number-one *L.A. Times* bestseller—and *From Survive to Thrive*, a number-one Amazon bestseller.

He earned his master's degree from Lehigh University and has received honorary doctorates from Northwest University, William Jessup University, and Baptist University of the Americas.

Rodriguez serves as the senior pastor of New Season Church, one of America's fastest-growing megachurches and number thirteen on "Newsmax's Top 50 Megachurches in America," with campuses in Los Angeles and Sacramento, California, where he resides with his wife, Eva, and their three children.

For more information, please visit:

 PastorSam.com

RevSamuelRodriguez

@pastorsamuelrodriguez

@nhclc